Life as I Know It...
So Far

Mandy Osterhaus Ream

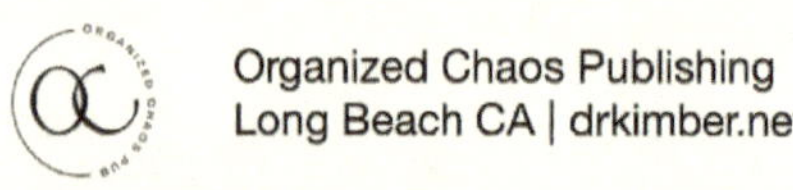

Organized Chaos Publishing
Long Beach CA | drkimber.net

While stories in the book are true, some names and identifying information may have been changed to protect the privacy of individuals.

Cover design and image composition: Andrea Bowers
Interior Design: Chris Sowers

ISBN 979-8-2182339-4-5 (print)
ISBN 979-8-9870881-2-8 (digital)

Printed in the United States of America

Library of Congress Cataloging in Publication Data
A catalog record for this book is available from the Library of Congress.

To Mom and Dad, my biggest fans.

Essays

Introduction

My stomach turns as I walk through the library stacks to the study area. *What am I doing? What am I doing? What am I doing?* chirps in my head like a small bird mocking me from a tall branch. This is the voice that has kept me from doing this for many years.

There are enough books already. Why do you want to add to them? What do you have to say? This will never happen. You'll be like all those characters in all those novels with unrequited dreams. Such a privilege, to dream.

All this reverberates in my brain as I take my seat. I am here despite the voices.

I am here to spite them.

With my fiftieth birthday mere months away, I am taking stock of my life dreams and decisions as I do around every milestone birthday.

At thirty, I was desperate for children, children that were not coming as easily as I'd hoped they would. I spent my thirties working through infertility and celebrating, at thirty-five, the birth of my first son and then my second two years later. I spent the end of my thirties caring for these boys and wondering what a Down Syndrome diagnosis meant for my younger son, wondering what is meant for me.

At forty, I ushered in the decade with grand hopefulness that I had done enough work on myself that I could put my inner battles and issues in the rearview mirror and look ahead to self-actualization.

Ah, the idealism of youth.

I began to dream in my forties of returning to my life as a professor. Like wanting children, it became a bit desperate, this desire. But it also became another dream realized when I returned to the classroom at forty-four.

And, once again, I find myself hopeful as I look to a new decade with a new dream. With the new dream comes great doubt and familiar questioning. It holds a different vulnerability with this fresh declaration that I want to put things out into the world, things from inside me, things describing the journey of being human. Things to which a reader might say, *Yes. I feel that too. I have seen the world from a similar vantage point. I am so glad to know I'm not alone.*

I write to feel less alone, like many of us, in the muck of life and in the triumphs. I want to share and share broadly. Preferably on the page *and* into a microphone.

But dreams are funny things. Along with the vulnerability they hold so much hope, risk, and surprise.

I wanted children so deeply and explored many avenues to create a family. And during the years while I waited, I had opportunities to nurture people in other ways, to care for students in my classroom, a classroom I left for a time when my children arrived.

Then, I wanted to be in the classroom again so deeply that when I returned it felt like I was once again using an arm that had been dangling at my side for a decade. But during the years when I wasn't teaching in a formal setting, I taught in other ways, to my boys, to small groups of women, and to myself.

Writing is the same way. I can't not write. It happens whether I have a publishing goal or a speaking engagement or it's a lonely Saturday morning with just me and my laptop. Like I found ways to nurture and mother and teach, I find ways to write. I have been doing this for a long time now. But much like the arrival of babies or a new teaching position, I am eager for the writing to materialize into something more.

Wanting more is scary.

Audacious.

One of the scariest things about dreaming is declaring the dream out loud in the first place, out in the world where the voices might mock and attack. But also, perhaps, to celebrate and applaud. I am finding strength in using the voices of doubt and questioning as rocks to grab onto on the mountain of this dream as I climb.

And quietly, often without warning or fanfare, the voices in my head change from doubt to encouragement. They whisper, *keep climbing, keep climbing, keep climbing*.

And I hear, *keep dreaming*.

Part I – *Life Lessons*

Hocking Phony Baked Goods

It started simply. I needed a summer job in college and the owner of a farmer's market stand needed help. It never dawned on me that I would navigate the biggest ethical dilemma of my life at twenty-one.

My employer was a large woman in size, personality and desperation as she struggled to make enough money baking for farmer's markets to keep her house in rural Virginia. Recently divorced with a young teenage daughter, she supported herself by selling quality baked goods in the Washington DC suburbs.

Her food was delicious.

Muffins moist and flavorful. Golden-crusted pies. I often brought them home for my family and friends, proud of my sales.

When I was first hired for the position that summer, I met Mrs. C before dawn in different parking lots to sell her muffins and pies. I arranged the tables. I displayed her wares. I hung the "HOMEMADE" sign on the awning.

And, I unsuspectingly sold previously frozen Sara Lee pies and re-wrapped Otis Spunkmeyer muffins.

After a month at the markets, I was invited to work a few afternoons a week at her house to assist with the actual baking. I relished this trusted position because the hours were good and few people worked both "in the field" *and* behind the scenes.

I quickly understood why she didn't want the front-of-the-house workers to meet the ones in the back.

In her garage-turned-bakery, two worlds collided—that of skilled baker with cunning counterfeiter.

In the walk-in freezers sat a few legitimate homemade pies alongside boxes and boxes of frozen ones, ready to be thawed and "enhanced" with egg-wash and finger-crimped edges.

What had once been an above-board bakery business, had turned into a darker industrial machine when my employer needed to increase productivity to save her house but was unable to bake from scratch enough items to meet demand.

Used tea bags dried above the sink in her kitchen waiting to be reused in her meager efforts to save money.

This was a crossroads between survival and ethics. Did I want to participate?

You see, there are strict Farmer's Market rules that reasonably require a baker to make food from scratch. There is an understandable expectation that signs reading "Homemade" should mean just that.

I felt incredible compassion for this woman and her

daughter. I wanted to support her and her efforts. But late one Friday night getting ready for the weekend, as I unwrapped the Otis Spunkmeyer muffins and rewrapped them in clear plastic before applying her business labels, I began to question my integrity. I was waffling between staying to help and getting out of there as fast as I could.

This final straw made my decision clear.

I arrived at work one afternoon and was urgently instructed to remove all the contraband in the garage and take it to a back bedroom where Mrs. C's daughter was covering the piles with blankets.

On my second trip to the back of her house, I noticed a car coming down the long driveway and then two very serious individuals approaching the house. As they passed a front window to the door, I was tiptoeing through the kitchen with an armload of boxes.

The Farmer's Market police.

If one hangs a sign that reads HOMEMADE, those pies sure as hell better be homemade.

Makes sense.

With my anxiety through the roof, as both a rule-follower and a people-pleaser, I completed my last trip to the back of the house, grabbed my keys and headed toward a side door.

I recall one last encounter with Mrs. C as I made my exit. It included both a shaming rebuke, "You're going to leave me too?" and an eye-roll as I said, "I'm sorry." I may have even muttered, "Good luck" but I was practically running, afraid she would come flying out after me.

It was a long drive home on two-lane Virginia country

roads.

Eventually, my speed and my heart rate decelerated but I stayed swimming in utter bafflement, both at what had just happened and that the circumstances weren't clear cut to me. There was the obvious ethical breach *and* the despairing Jean Valjean-like attempts to provide.

Even though I quit that day, I didn't move away from wrestling in the tension. I stayed open to the possibility that struggling to survive leads to crazy things. I was willing to consider the messiness. And I've been open to messy ever since.

Oh, and if you happen upon a frozen Sara Lee pie, they're delicious. Cook as instructed and I'll show you how to finger crimp the edges.

A Conversation with Jealousy

(First published in Pink Panther Magazine, March 2022)

Jealousy has been on my mind for a long time, almost as long as I've been a jealous person, and I'm ready to get rid of it. But I'm not sure exactly how to do this. Is there a way to package it up, put a stamp on it and mail it far away? Is there a magic formula? A certain amount of meditation or journaling? What is the secret? I don't want it to be a part of my regular experience anymore. I am ready for it to hit the road.

When I talked about this with a close friend, he suggested one possible way to remove Jealousy from my life was to first talk to it and ask it why it is here.

And I thought, what now?

This was advice he received from his counselor who encouraged him to have conversations with parts of himself.

"Like parts of your body?" I asked, not clear on the concept.

"No. Parts of me like my anxiety or my anger," he replied.

When certain things arise in him, like fury, he has a conversation with it. A check-in. A Q&A session to find out what those parts need. He asks what is triggering their appearance at that particular moment. His therapist went one step further, encouraging him to literally pull out two chairs, one for himself and one for the part of him he was going to address, like anger, and talk to it directly.

The chair part threw me a bit, but I was intrigued.

A conversation with parts of oneself. This was a new take on self-examination, something to which I have been dedicated (maybe fixated on) for much of my adult life, motivated by the idea "the unexamined life is not worth living," often attributed to Socrates. The goal of my introspection has been a deep desire to understand my motivations and biases, often unconscious, and to uncover blind spots with the hopes that I could heal my broken places and be kinder to myself.

Self-examination often requires excavation of my inner life, digging deep into places that have long been ignored or hidden. But like understanding the movement of tectonic plates and fault lines to better grasp earthquakes and the destruction they can create, I am seeking to uncover the fault lines that cause certain things on the surface (like Jealousy) to shake my relationships and hinder my ability to live well.

But I had never thought about having actual conversations with parts of me.

Then, I found myself in the midst of a particularly

jealous day, where Jealousy was attempting a toxic take-over. Talking to it suddenly seemed like a compelling idea and I decided to find out why it was there. What ensued was a much more intellectual and clinical interaction with Jealousy than I've had in the past.

"Why are you here?" I asked Jealousy.

I was surprised when it answered back.

"Because there isn't enough," it said.

"Enough what?" I asked.

"Of everything," Jealousy replied.

Oh, I wondered, is this connected to the scarcity mind-set that Brene Brown and others talk about? Is it the idea that resources or good things – friends, happiness, good-ness – are scarce and so I must grab all I can? Or the ex-perience of seeing another person with something I don't have and feeling Jealousy erupt because it believes there isn't enough available in the world for more than one per-son to have it?

Years ago, I talked about the presence of Jealousy, spe-cifically in my friendships, with a therapist who helped me survive my thirties. He described friendships as additive, suggesting if one of my friends had another friend, it wasn't taking something away from me, but rather it was adding a relationship to my friendship that already ex-isted. There was enough love to go around. His idea was a radical departure from the scarcity mindset that con-sumed me. I wanted to be a clear *best* friend or *only* friend. And if I wasn't, then the relationship was marked by scar-city and deprivation. I was the one being deprived.

When my therapist first shared this, I was immediately

reminded of a time when my husband and I visited old friends and their five children. While we were chatting in the living room, their youngest stomped down the stairs and dramatically threw herself into her mom's lap and wailed, "There isn't enough love for me. You only love Cash." She was referring to child number four, the sibling above her. We adults chuckled at her precocious observation. Her mom just smiled as she gently stroked her hair. "Of course there's enough love for you," she murmured.

I too smiled at this exchange, but I felt uneasy. Listening to this little girl nudged something deep in my soul and reflected a similar fear I, too, was holding onto. There isn't enough love *for me*, along with many other things, so I am jealous when others seem to have more...of just about anything.

Sometimes this perception of scarcity is connected to a belief that there is some attainable whole (some faith frameworks might say Heaven, Nirvana, the Kingdom of God) where all of this is possible but we just have to wait for the whole to be achieved after we die.

Perhaps the scarcity mindset is behind the toxic lure of social media – that we present a picture of an implied whole. We pretend we have it all. Edit out the lack and the limits. And others believe we have achieved a perfect whole...we have achieved the unachievable.

And this may be one secret of Jealousy, or the secret to getting away from it once and for all – understanding there is no achievable completeness where one person has absolutely everything. We all have and we all don't have.

I remember thinking about this in a women's small

group I was a part of for many years, where Jealousy would rear its head inside me quickly, ferociously, and without warning. Each one of us lacked something most of the others possessed. And each of us had qualities the others didn't. Sometimes, when I would feel myself coveting something one of the women was talking about, I would remind myself that I possessed other things that she didn't. None of us had it all. And generally, I concluded this was okay. But I was baffled at how I continually forgot the obvious awareness: no one has it all, and yet how unconsciously motivated I was by the fallacy that "having it all" was attainable.

These observations were tricky, like I was dancing on a precipice of them being either helpful and insightful or quite destructive – where I could at any moment fall into a canyon of measurement and comparison – "Well, I have this and she doesn't." Point for me. And I didn't want that exercise to devolve into a mental zero-sum game of one-upmanship.

In a more centered, life-giving perspective I might begin to feel jealous of my friend and realize that although I don't have X or possess Y, I have P and Q. The distribution of things, qualities, as well as hardships and challenges, is not cosmically equal. On my best days, I might even celebrate the great gifts my friend has, even if the same things aren't in my world as well. I want to be a person who celebrates my friends.

My conversation with Jealousy continued. I said, "I think you're looking at *enough* all wrong. I think you've defined it as having *everything*."

This part of the conversation with Jealousy was also informed by another conversation with a wise friend. A new, wise friend. (I highly recommend wise friends. They are a true gift.) This new friend, Bronwen, was introduced to me by a very close mutual friend, Carrie. Carrie, also a cherished wise one, thought that Bronwen and I should meet and get to know one another. Over dinner one night with our husbands, Bronwen toasted our friend Carrie, thanking her for her magnanimity at sharing one dear friend with another.

Now, this language might read a little silly. Share one's friend? We are adults. Free agents. Except, that is not how I often hold people in my heart. I often hold them possessively. She's *my* friend. And if this friend goes on to be friends with someone else, I will lose something. My new friend Bronwen echoed this experience in her own life. When Jealousy takes hold of friendships it can be very difficult to share.

Bronwen and I talked about this on a recent walk when I asked her about the dinner together and her relationship with Jealousy. (It is amazing to find a new friend open to answering questions like, what's your relationship with Jealousy?)

In her answer, she offered a beautiful insight from the course "The Artist's Way." She suggested Jealousy might be signaling to us the presence of a deep longing for something, and the deep longing is good. The crunchy part is that when the deep longing emerges, we let Jealousy take over and then seek to destroy, attack, or put down people or things we can't have. Bronwen continued by saying one powerful response to the deep longing is to try and offer it something.

I might be jealous of friends who have swimming pools in their backyards, the ability to fully submerge their bodies in cool water anytime they want. And in the sophisticated workings of a wounded inner world, I can make having a pool bad somehow or let Jealousy fuel self-pity. Another option is to dip myself in the ocean, which is a mile away. (And that sentence might invoke Jealousy for another person.) Or I can draw a cool bath. Or I can call one of my friends who knows my deep psychological need to be in water and ask if I can come float.

Sometimes I might just pour myself a glass of ice water to drink while I have another conversation with Jealousy. And, in this discussion I say to Jealousy, I see you have a deep longing but also isn't it great that my friend has a pool? I want my friends to get good things.

This is a very true statement. I want good things for people I love.

One difficult element to this new dynamic with Jealousy is it seems to have amnesia.

It requires many conversations. And sometimes the conversations are exhausting. Sometimes it takes far less effort to just let Jealousy have its way with me until it tires out and I can move on with my day. But I have noticed that Jealousy unchecked doesn't seem to just peter out or go away. Jealousy might get tired and stop for a rest but it is always breathing and alive. Unchecked it can take over my being, like a house engulfed in flames started by a forgotten pot on a hot gas stove.

When I am too tired for an in-depth conversation with Jealousy, sometimes I simply acknowledge its presence. "I see you there," I say. "Just stay where you are and we'll talk about this later." The simple act of awareness can diffuse its power a bit.

And I'm noticing, that with each acknowledgment and conversation, Jealousy has just a little less to say. Its arguments aren't as persuasive as they once were. As it shrinks, there is a bit more room in my soul for the contentment and the celebrating of others I long for.

Celebrating feels so much better than being jealous. And it requires far fewer conversations.

Objects of My Affection

She lived at the top of my street and I idolized her. She was the star and I, the groupie. A fan club of one.

1983.

Just five years older, Laura was everything I wasn't. In my eyes, she had it all. Beautiful and magnetic, she was a popular student at the local high school, both winning Homecoming Queen her senior year and singing her heart out as the lead in the school's musical production of whatever was popular at the time. She had long brown hair with full curls that supported tall, fluffy bangs and perfect feathers along her face; aqua-netted hair pushed out over her ears.

I, on the other hand, was decidedly rooted in the awkward stages of late adolescence. I was trying to ready myself for the precarious journey into the teen world. I was growing out my Dorothy Hamill haircut, which had been a desperate attempt at getting my curly hair to shape-shift into glorious feathered hair like Laura's, not knowing how to smooth my frizz any other way.

Laura was an expert. And I, like an apprentice taking notes from the master, studied her, learning the ways of 1980s teendom.

I memorized her walk and smile and how she constantly maintained her coif with a ubiquitous brush in her back pocket. On one rare occasion, she took me shopping and I watched as she reapplied lipstick before leaving the dressing room, double-checking that her feathers were flying just so.

Sometimes I was invited into the inner sanctum, sitting on her bedroom floor, watching her get ready for some exciting evening out. The words alone, "evening out," elicited wonderment. Other times I helped her with household chores, just wanting to be in her orbit.

It was all so thrilling.

But nothing took my breath away more than the popped collars of her vibrant Izod Lacoste pique cotton polo shirts. Alligator present and accounted for.

The Izod Lacoste polos didn't just complete her perfect look. They were the statement pieces that said, "I have arrived." They declared, "This is the best time of my life and I am going to mark this moment in full color." My mouth still waters as I envision the vast rainbow of Izod shirts hanging in her closet; various hues of pinks and greens and yellows, like rows of sherbet ice cream at Baskin Robbins.

It was my glimpse at this pot of gold that slowly opened me up to the world of fashion, a world I was very, very far away from. A world I have still never fully entered into, but one I would covetously study at a distance.

Not quite in middle school, I was still running around the neighborhood in practical clothes designed to weather tree climbs and bike rides. But I was becoming more aware of certain things I would like to add to my wardrobe. Izod Lacoste alligator polo shirts were at the top of my list.

My parents, in their mid-30s, were tending to us three kids while working and finishing degrees. Fashion was not a concern. Time was limited and we were more Kmart shoppers and less, well, less of wherever Izod Lacoste polo shirts were sold at the time. My parents were not interested in my need to keep up with Joneses, or in this case, the Lauras.

Some of this was economics.

Even when my mom and I did go to the mall, the coffers just weren't full enough to allow for my burgeoning fashion needs. When Jordache jeans made their way into my 6th-grade classroom, I knew enough to not ask. I eventually did, however, save up money to purchase my first, and only, pair of Guess jeans when they surpassed Jordache as the pinnacle of jean success.

But what I considered the most prized fashion statement of the mid-'80s eluded me. Izod Lacoste polo shirts remained squarely out of reach.

Then, one day, Laura said I could borrow a piece of the cherished treasure. A bright pink one. The dark green alligator even more vivid in contrast. The pink one was my favorite and because Laura owned so many, I imagined she wouldn't miss this one. I was desperate to be given, not loaned, this prized possession.

However, it remained decidedly a loan, and wearing it for one day was like dipping into a bag of perfectly salted potato chips. One day, like one chip, is simply insufficient. I tried to cherish that one day anyway.

Wearing the Pink Izod Lacoste polo shirt with the alligator straightened my shoulders, my chin extended with pride. My no-style curly hair was in the shadows of the radiating color on my body. I luxuriated in the pique cotton feel and relished the sensation of the collar just below my ears.

And then, I had to give the shirt back.

After Laura's senior year, she packed up a car and went off to college. A few years later my family moved to California. Our paths never crossed again.

Now in my 40s, it seems every few years a friend (or me) throws an 80's party, and sometimes I have even worn an Izod Lacoste pique cotton polo shirt found on eBay. For a fleeting moment, I am transported back to the days where I was the awkward 11, 12, 13-year-old trying to find my footing. And I am reminded of the kindness of an older girl who took me under her wing.

But, like the 80s parties themselves, the nostalgia fades, the feelings dissipate. The shirts don't hold the same luster. They are lacking one key element.

While these shirts are still available at Macy's and on eBay as vintage wear, I long for their paradoxical 1980s existence where they were both everywhere and exclusive at the same time.

I want the Izod Lacoste alligator polo shirt to be the statement piece of decades ago with the same just-out-of-reach allure. I also want to once again feel the visceral caterpillar-like transformation that happened when I donned that precious item; to experience the confidence evoked by the vibrant, colorful display. I want to feel the moment in time when I was on the cusp of a new chapter and it held such promise.

And yes, I believe a shirt can do all that.

Don't Catch What They're Throwing

Several years ago, I was with a group of volunteers celebrating the completion of a successful community event for over 1,000 people. As we wrapped up the night, counted the money, and inventoried unclaimed Silent Auction items, we realized we were all exhausted from our efforts and decided to finish up the following week.

I returned after the weekend to help attendees pay for their auction items when a woman came in to share a critique she had heard about our work. She reported that a festival attendee had made a passing comment and she wanted to relay it to me. "This man said, 'Would've been nice to get a call about my prize Friday night,'" she recounted.

"The nerve!" I thought.

Expletives flooded my thoughts, my blood pressure started to rise, and anger mounted as I began rehearsing a snide reply to this ungrateful, narrow-minded, selfish narcissist while brainstorming where this man could put his prize.

Then, from out of nowhere, I remembered a random story about monkeys who throw shit at people. Suddenly I was flooded by an epiphany about the similarities between monkeys and humans. It was rather alarming.

You see, monkeys, specifically chimpanzees, throw their feces at people and we humans do the same thing. Although we sophisticated beings add an extra step. We try to catch it.

One human throws shit and another person catches it, often unconsciously, instead of stepping aside and maybe even walking away.

At that moment in the volunteer room, it dawned on me: This guy JUST THREW SHIT AT THIS WOMAN, AND SHE CAUGHT IT!

Whatever limitations or hang-ups the disgruntled man had going on in his life, not getting notified about winning a prize the night of the event was very frustrating to him. Then, he bundled up his negative emotions about it and lobbed it, his issue (his feces in this metaphor), at the woman he passed in the hallway.

This happens all the time.

Recently I was feeling particularly stressed about things in both my parenting and professional life. As my frustration increased, I rolled it up and lobbed it at my husband, who was standing nearby. My shit had nothing to do with him, but I wanted to direct it somewhere and he was a convenient target. One technical term for shit-throwing is "projection." Very easy to do and often completely unconscious, which also adds to the convenience.

We also see people throwing shit at each other on social media, in the news, on the freeways. And the people they're aiming for? They freak out. React. Catch the shit. Shape it with their hands. Internalize some of it before taking aim to throw it back.

And, here's one more layer to add to the complexity of it all. I did not hear the original comment first-hand from the man. I did not catch his shit directly. I caught his shit from the other volunteer who told us about the comment.

I heard the comment third-hand. Man throws shit. Woman catches it. Woman then mushes it around with her hands, forms a ball, and throws it at me. I catch it. And, to make it more interesting, the first woman added some of her issues to the shit (adding our shit, such as feelings of inadequacy that we didn't do a good job, issues about not feeling appreciated for the hard work we put in, etc., etc.) so it became a bigger ball of shit. And when I caught it, I added some of my own issues too before I got ready to throw it back at her or pass it on to someone else.

And this is what separates us from the monkeys; not opposable thumbs. It's catching the shit.

Of course, there is another option.

We don't catch it.

Instead of catching the shit, we could move out of the way and let it drop. Here's what it looks like if we don't catch what is thrown at us; if we don't collude with another person that his or her stuff is about us. The man throws his comment, "would've been nice…" at the woman and she steps out of the way, letting it land on the floor. Even if the first woman wasn't able to just move away from the shit, my friend and I could have chosen this alternative.

But what might this actually look like?

I see a person is frustrated about something. Maybe he's unable to consider all the factors that kept him from receiving his prize the night of the event. He might even try and make it my fault or my problem: incompetent Raffle/Silent Auction chairs; women; People taller than 5'4". But those are his issues. I know that we were working hard and there were some circumstances beyond our control. I know that we were part of a dedicated volunteer group of women who often felt like we were working on fumes. I don't have to catch this man's accusation or take on his vitriol. I can just step out of the way and let it fall next to me.

Of course, people shouldn't throw shit at you. Why am I even typing this sentence? But it happens. Monkeys throw shit. People project their issues onto others. We can't control this part of human interaction. But we can control our response. We read about this a lot. Consider what we can control. And catching shit is just one of those things.

Of course, there is still one important element to all of this. Even if I don't catch shit being thrown, it still stinks. Even if I walk quickly away, the stench lingers in my nostrils. It can churn something inside of me that makes me uncomfortable and that discomfort can be hard to deal with. But often this is far less toxic than if I begin to interact with the feces headed my way. And sometimes it takes a lot of energy to realize the shit in the air is his shit and not mine. I can smell it. I hate the smell. But that's all. Leave it there.

There is one other radical possibility, and only a possibility if other certain criteria are met like boundaries and no presence of imminent danger.

Sometimes, we can turn back to the monkey, the person, and TOSS BACK EMPATHY AND KINDNESS. We might gently say, "Hey, I see you've thrown some shit. How are you doing? Why are you throwing shit? Don't you know, we're all in this together?" (I've seen this done.) It's almost like seeing the shit and throwing back a Febreeze mist.

Sometimes the person catches this. And, sometimes the person lets grace and kindness fall on the floor. That's not under our control.

Sometimes we just start by reminding ourselves again and again: I don't have to catch the shit. I don't have to catch the shit. I don't have to catch the shit.

The Healing Powers of the Fuck-It Bucket

In my early thirties, when a person is still too young to get calls like this, one of my oldest and dearest childhood friends called from across the country to tell me she had cancer.

Advanced cervical cancer. As a busy mom of three young kids, with a husband gone for long stretches for work, she had missed the early signs and was now facing the unfaceable. Despite the distance, I kicked into high gear to send love and support in any way I could.

My friend began the grueling process of chemo, etc, etc., and spent long hours in bed. I thought, what would be helpful in the moments when she wanted to distract her mind? She was a deeply spiritual person and found solace in worship music and Bible verses but sometimes the "Praying Through Cancer" books got tiresome, so I sent her some of my favorites at the time, "Bridget Jones' Diary," "Nanny Diaries" and "The Devil Wears Prada." The first I found laugh-out-loud funny and well, laughter is the best medicine.

Years later, I received another call. From another friend who had just experienced a seizure and learned it was from astrocytoma in her brain. The mother of two young children, she was anticipating major brain surgery and a long recovery. During one of the early visits to see her at Cedars Sinai in Los Angeles, I noticed under the television a small plaque that read, "Comedy Central, Channel 113."

Hmmm. Noteworthy that the hospital would highlight one channel on the neurosurgery wing and that channel was comedy.

When I next visited her in the hospital, I told her I would bring a chapter from my favorite book for a bedside reading. And she was game. Still woozy and recovering, she smiled as I embarked on, "Jesus Shaves" from David Sedaris' book "Me Talk Pretty One Day." I did not anticipate that a number of our friends would be settled into the room and there was quite an audience present chuckling along as I read.

I am someone who uses humor as a defense mechanism, to divert from hard things. I'm quite good at it. But over the years I have also developed the ability to sit in challenging places and put humor aside. For my first friend, I helped her to the restroom when a nurse in the hospital wasn't available. For my second friend, I held a tissue to the side of her nose when her right side was temporarily paralyzed from the tumor and she couldn't blow her nose sufficiently.

I didn't use humor to completely escape the realities of what was happening to my friends, but I wasn't afraid to access it in some of the darker moments.

Enter my purple wig.

A third friend spent a year treating breast cancer, from which she fully recovered. But it was a brutal year. Unlike my other friends, she lived nearby and I was able to pop in to bring flowers or just say hi. One morning, I came by for a visit after she had lost the final bits of hair and was sporting knit caps. I thought this a perfect opportunity to show support and knocked on her door wearing my cute purple wig cut in a short bob. It was itchy and got uncomfortable quickly and some of that was just the point.

She too was uncomfortable and the wig made her smile. For my friends who were spending day-in and day-out in the throes of illness and treatment, sometimes you just need a purple wig and a funny book or a special bucket.

Here we come to the Fuck-It Bucket.

In the book I mentioned above, "Me Talk Pretty One Day," David Sedaris writes about his brother who has a panacea for hard times: The Fuck-It Bucket. It's quite simple actually, "a plastic pail filled with jawbreakers and bite-size candy bars. When shit brings you down, just say 'fuck it,' and eat yourself some motherfucking candy."

It is a unique person who decides to give this bucket to a sick or hurting friend (if I do say so myself). It is an equally unique person who receives this bucket.

And generally, the two are bonded for life.

This was the case for our office administrator at the

elementary school my boys attended and where I served on the PTA board for a number of years. Close to the beginning of one school year, this friend learned she had advanced cancer. She was a remarkable presence in the front office, offering care and wisdom to many who came in. We were all distraught. With her ribald sense of humor and quick wit, she was a perfect recipient of the bucket, which I gave to her at school one day. (Although I labeled it in code because of, well, the kids.)

There is a certain risk that the bucket or a wig might be perceived as dismissive of the real pain in these stories. But in concert with a listening ear, foot rubs in the hospital, and tears together in bed, humor can offer a powerful release.

I recently shared the Fuck-It Bucket idea with a friend caring for a dying mother in a toxic environment. I wasn't able to deliver a bucket to her but I walked her through the process of making one.

I also listened and said over and over, "Shit, this is really hard."

So, the bucket shouldn't come by itself. But a bucket or book or wig can serve as a different kind of connection, a life-line that says, I see you are still alive and to be alive is to laugh sometimes.

And if you have that person in your life who you think a worthy recipient of the Fuck-It Bucket, I highly recommend it. And if you also wear a purple wig when you deliver it, well, all the better.

Who thought jumping was a good idea?

I comfortably ascended, marveling at all the choices I had made leading me to this moment climbing a thirty-five-foot telephone pole in the middle of Missouri. It was a beautiful day to explore all that the camp offered by way of team-building exercises. However, my enthusiasm for the task quickly drained from my body as I neared the top of the pole and realized the next step was going to be much harder than I first thought; seemingly impossible, in fact. What had been a fun afternoon quickly spiraled into a tornado of dark inner thoughts amidst a barrage of cruel self-attacking messages. I was eager to abort the mission and clamber down.

Clambering down was not an option.

This activity was a team-building / personal growth / face-your-fears kind of thing where participants are equipped with a harness and the instructions to climb to the top of a tall pillar. Once there, the climber is next supposed to place her feet on the small circle at the pinnacle, without handles or pulls to steady herself. Finally, the challenge is complete when she launches herself into the air towards a trapeze swing about five feet (maybe one thousand feet) away from the perch on which she stands.

A few in my group immediately volunteered to go first. One girl, in her late teens like me, confidently began the climb with ease. We were a group spending the summer between semesters of college to work at a sprawling sleep-away sports camp outside of Branson, Missouri and this was our afternoon off to explore some of the camp's exciting outdoor activities like the ropes course, the zipline, and this pole climb.

I cheered along with my fellow staffers as our friend neared the end of the pole. Once there, in one sure movement, she placed her feet on the small flat top and steadily raised herself until she was fully standing. Then she assessed her marker and jumped out, grabbing the bar of the trapeze and swinging gleefully before signally she was ready to be lowered back to earth.

"That was so fun!" she exclaimed as she unhooked the belts.

Cool. I thought. I was ready to try, adrenaline already building in my body as I hooked on the safety ropes and bounded towards the first rungs on the pole. I generally liked challenging myself, having left my home for the summer to head out to the middle of the country where I didn't know a soul. This particular undertaking seemed a little out of my usual experience, but I was familiar with much of the camp / team / you-go-girl expectations, and up I went.

It was fun to climb as I stretched my long limbs to reach each handle. Around me, the thick Missouri woods extended out in all directions. I loved passing the forest ceiling in all its vast, thick, green density. I felt strong, exhilarated as I moved, reminded of fond childhood memories of summer days spent in trees.

Then, as I reached the last foothold, I realized there was just one more rung between me and the apex of the pole. If I advanced further, the top of my body would extend out into nothingness. I paused, the reality of the next steps washing over me. Exhilaration crumpled into fear.

The woods beneath me fell away as my vision myopically focused on the tiny eight-inch disk in front of me onto which I was now supposed to place my massive size eleven feet. . .with only air to grab. Suddenly, the harness strapped onto me earlier seemed like nothing more than dental floss loosely tucked into my pockets for all I imagined it would help if I fell. And, I was now quite angry with the girl who had gone before me, furious at her confidence and the dexterity with which she completed this task.

Um, I don't think I want to do this anymore, I thought.

"I may just climb down," I reluctantly called to the group below, chuckling a little as I said it, attempting to use one of my well-honed defense mechanisms, humor.

"No!" they cheered with enthusiasm. "Go on!" You've got this! Go, Mandy!" they yelled, enjoying their role as cheerleaders.

I wondered if this was exactly how the drama was supposed to play out. Perhaps the jumper before me hadn't fully embraced all the parts of this challenge, completing the task a little too quickly (which I now hated her for, misleading me so brazenly) and I was now going to live this more true to the expectations of the activity, as if the rules of team-building were written on the plaque describing just how the challenge should go.

Instructions for Pole Climb Life Lesson Activity: Participant climbs. She waffles. Team cheers and encourages. Participant musters her courage. She jumps. Team claps. Jumper learns life lesson. And scene.

It became increasingly clear, however, that my part in this drama was not going to play out to script either, the waffling turning to terror, terror that was starting to hijack my body as I once again reviewed the life decisions that got me into this asinine predicament.

I pushed myself upward, trying to figure out how in the world I was going to stand on this little shelf. It seemed physically impossible. I was taller than that damn, tiny girl before me. My feet were longer. That had to mean something. Maybe I wasn't the right size for this task. Surely the leaders knew this.

I forced myself up one more rung, a dull ache now starting in my temples; the corners of my eyes beginning to sting.

Bent over the microscopic platform I could see far below me my fellow camp-staffers down on the ground smiling, their cheers doing nothing to abate the tears that began to drop.

Our leader called up, "Now just put your feet on the top and stand up. No sweat. You've got this."

Yeah right, I thought, beginning to brainstorm bait-and-switch options where my so-called friends would all be distracted and I could quickly scramble down. A bear, perhaps? Bears were a real possibility in the area.

Miraculously, I pressed on. With what felt like violent shaking, I moved one foot up now in an extended stretch, uncertain I could actually bring the other to meet it. The pole began to sway ever so slightly with my movements.

Panic.

But the ache in my calf outweighed the anxiety-induced cramping in my stomach, so I attempted my second foot, sloth-like, until I could place it on the thin strip next to the first. There was nothing left to do but straighten my body, although remaining bent while clutching my legs for dear life seemed like the better option. So what if my feet were now going numb? I gradually uncurled my back one vertebra at a time, arms hovering just above my hips, convinced the quivering in my legs would knock me backwards into oblivion. Finally, I stood full height looking out over the Ozarks, reviewing what I had for breakfast, certain it was going to make an appearance at any minute.

"I'll start counting and you jump on three, okay?" Our leader called brightly.

Fuck you, I thought, words I so desperately wanted to scream but realized would result in my quick dismissal from this Christian camp if I did.

"Okaaaay," I squeaked back.

"One! Two..."

"Wait! Wait! I just need a minute!" I yelled.

There is no way I can do this, I thought.

How in the world was I going to move my now paralyzed limbs out towards that swing? Hadn't I already achieved something getting to this damn point?

"I'm just going to climb down," I called to the group below, signaling to the people holding the safety line attached to my harness. "I think I'm good," now imagining a Cirque du Soleil type body contortion to get my hands and feet safely back around the pole, waiting for rescue. Helicopter perhaps?

"No! No!" They yelled back.

"You've got this! You can do it!" They exclaimed with all the confidence of people who are firmly set on solid ground, the enthusiasm masking smug judgment of those who had already completed the challenge. At least, I thought I registered smug judgment in some of their ant-sized faces.

"No, really. I get the lesson. I'm coming back down," I replied, now fully engulfed in desperation.

"No!" They yelled together, playing their parts in this drama with expertise. They, the chorus, were still energized by the hope that the hero (the anti-hero?) would also faithfully complete her part – triumph over adversity and leap to her reward. (I was beginning to think a trapeze swing was not that great of an incentive.)

I also thought I detected their enthusiasm beginning to wane, impatience creeping into their voices, boredom setting in. It was becoming difficult to separate my cohort from the sneering voices in my head. The pace of this overcoming-personal-fears was going much slower than the expertly edited pieces on inspirational prime-time television shows.

"Ok," I called, choking on the sound. "I'll count for myself."

"One...two..."

Pause.

"Hold on...I don't think I can..."

"Come on already," I thought I heard one say, but I was increasingly only aware of the pounding in my skull.

I was having difficulty remembering the point of all of this as the blood drained from my head, leaving me foggy and swaying like the pole above the tree line.

The taunters below, for that is now what their voices had become in my mind, would have none of that. I wasn't playing the game right. The instructions for the activity did not include: She climbs. She waffles. She freaks out at the top of a telephone pole and has to be airlifted to the hospital after choking on her own vomit.

It would be years before I had the help of Brene Brown's call to overcoming shame, "Daring Greatly," and now on this precipice, I was equipped only with some rudimentary tools for survival that were quickly thrown aside in the wake of shame and failure. I had done some work on risk-taking and character-building, but I was beginning to wonder what was the importance of character anyway? I'm sure I had enough to get by. Why did I need more? Or perhaps I didn't have any at all. Perhaps I was just a superficial shell of a person who smiled a lot with great vivacity only to hide the nothingness inside; the black hole of self that couldn't even complete a simple task like jumping out to a stupid trapeze.

Resignation. I was going to climb down.

"Sorry. Never mind. I'm good," I declared again. "I've learned some things," I announced. "I'm climbing down?" I pleaded in more of a question than a statement.

One last time the chorus erupted with their lines, "No! No! You're doing great. Just jump. We've got you!" Were some of the girls studying their fingernails? Did she just stifle a yawn? Was that disdain in her tone? There was disdain in my head. The voices in my head were getting louder with vicious attacks and angry criticism of me.

"Why do you have to be so dramatic anyway? You're weak and ridiculous. This isn't that hard you moron. Those people down there aren't cheering you on. They are simply eager to get on with it. You are taking up way too much time in this afternoon of supposed fun."

More shame.

"Why can't you just climb, stand, jump, cheer and move on like the girl before you? Why are you so fragile and lame? This is safe. Just jump. There's nothing to be afraid of. The ropes are fine. What is wrong with you? Just jump already!"

The gnawing in my stomach wouldn't go away and I simply couldn't will my feet to push off from my perch. No amount of pleading, cajoling, or threatening from inside or out could launch me from this space. Tears ran and ran and ran, blurring the beautiful expanse out in front of me.

"Just jump already, you stupid idiot," the voice inside bullied me as I looked down at the long toes of my sneakers stiffened out into the abyss with nothing but air below them. My internal waffling now so exhausting I thought I might pass out.

What was the point here again? I wondered. How much more shame could I feel if I simply climbed back down?

"Just go already, Mandy. For god's sake, get on with it," the voice in my head said contemptuously.

Contempt. I felt such contempt. There was no triumph in this moment. No illumination of the strength I never knew I had. Just resignation that this was me, scared and crying 35 feet in the air, wishing I could have been the confident jumper, the strong one, the winner, the hero.

It was time for all of this to be over.

Then I just shuffled off into nothing, my feet simply not-standing any more instead of an intentional act of agency on my part.

A lurch in my stomach.

Falling.

A quick catch on the harness.

A smooth descent as the safety leads slowly released.

My head bent in shame as I landed.

With such a deflating end to this torturous experience, I imagined a few cursory pats on my back with exasperated exhales as the group moved on to the next activity. I had failed the challenge, never meeting the expectation of overcoming inner hurdles to reach self-actualization in the form of a gentle swing on a trapeze. So much time had been wasted coaxing me to jump I figured everyone was over it all by the time I rejoined them. I was certain my fellow camp-staffers would see it as a failure too and try to mask it as best they could while I slid off to the periphery of the group, attempting to collect any dignity I had left.

But as my feet touched the earth, something rather unexpected happened. I was immediately and overwhelmingly embraced in a group hug. And I wept.

"That was awful," I choked, trying to find a place for a laugh, uncomfortable in the huddle. Uncomfortable in the vulnerable exposure of all that had just transpired. Unable to understand the comfort and support in the midst of my humiliation. But the huddle just got tighter.

"You made it!" someone exclaimed.

Dizzyingly, I began to question reality.

Hold on. The voices in my head that so berated me for the last 300 days (or maybe 45 minutes) I was up there weren't actually saying what everyone was thinking? Shame was not the only option in this whole torturous experience? I might not actually be a failure, even if I didn't conquer this stupid, stupid challenge?

One reality of my time spent at the top of the 35-foot telephone pole was that I had used up all of our time. The last girls would have to try another day. So, we gathered our things and walked to the zip line. And as we headed to the next event, I considered new instructions for the pole climb; instructions specific to me.

Instructions for My Attempting the Pole Climb Activity: She climbs. She waffles. She hears voices that sound true but are really just telling lies. She hobbles off. She accepts she is loved anyway.

Simply Trying to Remember

I forget things. Many things. Like birthdays, that I am loved, to write Thank You notes, and that Icy Hot painfully burns my neck skin. But I have found one strategy that is remarkably effective in helping me remember. And I was reminded of this with the Icy Hot.

I wear the brunt of my stress in my neck and am often employing many types of relief. If I can't get to acupuncture, I try different home remedies like a heating pad or the Hypervolt or roll-on Icy Hot. This last one my husband suggested and the first time I used it, I lay moaning next to him in bed as it proceeded to burn my skin like a bad result from too much sun.

The night ended with me running cold water over my neck under the kitchen faucet.

A few months passed and once again my neck was hurting. And, being my forgetful self, I reached for the Icy Hot. That night, as I again leaned over the kitchen sink trying to rinse the ointment off, I berated myself for my forgetfulness and brainstormed better strategies for remembering. Then, I applied a solution that seemed the most straightforward.

A few weeks later, my son asked what might help his sore arm and my husband again suggested Icy Hot. I was sitting in the living room when I heard my son ask from the bathroom,

"Uh, Mom? Why does this say 'MANDY NO' on it?"

I had forgotten and was quickly reminded of the strategy I had used. I just wrote on the lid a very clear message to myself.

Mandy No.

This strategy was so effective that I decided to try it for other things, like remembering I am loved.

I am confoundedly quick to forget this. My husband tells me a lot, both that I am loved and that I forget. Part of this is because I have long cultivated the belief that love must be earned, and in this paradigm, I am generally not doing enough to receive it.

So, I made a small piece of jewelry at a friend's art workshop to better remember. She offered an evening class to make bracelets and led us through the activity of hammering letters into a narrow metal strip and then shaping it around our wrists.

My letters read SAYAL: "Simply Accept You Are Loved." I was amazed at how quickly this became a mainstay in my wardrobe, like a piece of armor I put on every morning.

Now, when I am getting dressed and the insecurity of

my clothing choices begins to choke out any energy I have for the day, I put on my bracelet to remind myself that I am loved no matter what goes on my body.

When I am preparing for my classes and feel the familiar taunts of the inner voice that say I am not good enough to be a professor, I look at my bracelet and remind myself that I am loved, first and foundationally, no matter how class goes.

When I question the activity levels of my children and if they are enrolled in enough after-school things, I glance at my wrist and see those letters that tell me first I am loved. Because the root of these doubts and questions is if I don't do enough that day, if I fail, I am not worthy of love. The bracelet reminds me that I am.

The bracelet has been such a successful, encouraging means of remembering, that I started writing things to remember on my other arm. When I selected a word for the New Year around which to focus my personal growth, I decided to write it on the inside of my arm with a sharpie.

In small black letters is the word "CHOOSE," reminding me I have agency in things that have long seemed like more objective reality than a choice I can make.

For instance, in my relationship with food. I can choose other ways to self-soothe besides french fries or cupcakes. Or in how I respond to the world around me. I can choose my reactions to things no matter the circumstances. Having the word spelled out on my inner arm serves as a constant hourly reminder.

Some of this I learned from my mother, who has many words in the places she occupies that announce things she wants to remember (and things she wants my dad to remember). Things like important deadlines or upcoming events. She keeps a supply of dry erase markers in convenient places all around the house, like in her bathroom, so she can write reminders on her mirror.

We were recently visiting my parents and there was a message written in dry erase marker on the inside of the microwave that said "Paper Towel" to remind my dad to cover the plates of food he is reheating. She has markers in her Volkswagen Beetle so she can write on the metal interior doors and dashboard.

My son caught the vision and wrote "Grady was here" on her glove box to remind my mother of his presence, a reminder she won't erase anytime soon.

Sometimes this method is more permanent. I see tattooed words on the arms of my students or the shoulders of friends. I, myself, got a tattoo in my early 40's to remember where I'm from. It is of the Dogwood, the Virginia state tree, an homage to and reminder of my roots even though I have now lived in California for over 20 years.

My husband likes the idea of having words out in the open as important reminders, and recently asked if we could remount an old sign we had hanging in our kitchen that I took down years ago when we remodeled. It read "Good Living."

This is a mantra we often say to one another or to our boys when we are in the midst of a particularly good moment, like hosting our neighbors for a barbecue or sitting at the beach on a warm Saturday afternoon, or enjoying dinner together at the kitchen counter. Simple moments that we want to anchor with a powerful reminder: This is Good Living.

This conversation prompted me to create a poster for my sons that describes the values of the Ream Team, a name we call ourselves. I hung it outside their bedroom doors as a reminder of what we are striving to be about as a family: Pay Attention, Be Generous, Practice Hospitality, Cultivate Empathy, Remember Good Living.

I see signs like this in other homes, words that are easily seen and serve as helpful reminders. Some are more general, "Live Laugh Love." Some very specific, "Peace to all who enter here," a reminder to both the guest and the host.

Sometimes it seems paradoxical, the need to write down what is obvious, things that we surely are the most apt to remember. This is precisely the point. There is so much noise and distraction and clutter in my head that can crowd out what is most important. I can't often rely on my brain alone to help me remember. I need something on my arm, on a lid, on the mirror to get me outside of my head, where there is too much going on.

One important detail I am quick to forget is how helpful my anti-anxiety medication is. When I start to feel better, to live with less anxiety, I wean myself off the medication thinking my mental health issues are finished. After a few weeks, I begin to feel more and more anxious, waking up early in the morning with heavy pressure on my chest, feeling the darkness closing in from my peripheral vision. Then, I return to the medication only to begin to feel better and forget that it is precisely because I am taking the medication that I feel this way.

During a recent talk with my doctor, he gently reminded me, again, that for some of us, these medications are like eyeglasses, necessary every day. And just like people don't question the need for eyeglasses when vision is blurry, I don't need to question the need for anti-anxiety medication when I experience daily, recurring anxiety that can make my reality out of focus.

In response to this, I told him my Icy Hot story and that perhaps I should write, "Mandy Yes" on the lid of the Trintellix.

He thought it was a great idea.

An Uber Angel

There are moments when personal limitations and the need for self-care are so crystal clear that dramatic choices need to be made. Choices like calling an Uber at nine o'clock at night and leaving a girls' weekend in wine country to go home, and home is an hour away.

Yes, it was an odd decision to go wine tasting in the middle of a dietary cleanse where I wasn't drinking alcohol. It was also difficult to leave for the weekend after a particularly hard fight with my husband that followed a long night of insomnia.

But I love the friends who were going and the wine tasting was just one part of a full weekend with other activities. So, I headed to wine country, sipped sparkling water, and served as the designated driver as my friends enjoyed dozens of pours.

Now, this particular California wine country is about an hour east of Los Angeles, and in August it is hot. Very hot. So despite not drinking wine, I started feeling a little woozy from the heat. And from my sleepless night. And from my emotional exhaustion from the conversation with my husband.

We did repair a little before I walked out the door, a repair that included a hug and reminder that we were going to make it. (We often quote to one another the wise sage Jon Bon Jovi, "We're gonna make it, I swear.") But all day after I left, I just wanted to settle in next to him and continue reconnecting.

I also didn't realize just how many pictures we were going to take, pictures where I often felt like the odd woman out next to my stunning friends; friends who appeared to be completely unaffected by the heat while I was visibly melting with each step.

Heat, exhaustion, marital disconnect, and melting are not great ingredients for a fun weekend.

After the wineries, the plan was to regroup in our shared room at the hotel and get ready for dinner and bar hopping. Before we reached the door, I quickly realized I was out of my league on the rallying-to-party front, too tired for anything but bed.

I felt tears welling up as we reached our room, a migraine starting in my temples, and nausea building in my stomach.

While they puttered around and checked social media, I pulled a blanket over me and took a migraine pill hoping to find some energy for the next phase of our evening. But all I wanted was my own bed.

It is one thing to want to go home, it is quite another to be an hour from home with no way to get there. There was also the building anxiety about bailing on the weekend.

As my friends discussed the evening plans, I suddenly announced through tears, I'm going home. I called an Uber, gathered my bags, and made my way to the door. They were kind, sympathetic even, albeit a little stunned. And I was focused on getting home.

There is a nervousness about getting into an Uber for an hour's drive home. I concluded if I felt an initial vibe of discomfort I would cancel. But when the car arrived, a kind gentleman opened the door.

"I am originally from Iran," he began as he pulled out of the hotel, "and I am a grandfather. Two grandchildren," he continued, pulling up pictures on his phone.

"I just started driving Uber after I sold my business. It was my business for over twenty years," he continued.

I was just so thankful there were no serial killer vibes and I settled into the seat, slowly relaxing in the air conditioning.

When he needed to stop for gas before the freeway, he bought me a Frappuccino. "For my new daughter" he said. I didn't tell him I wasn't only drinking water and kombuchas because of my cleanse, moved by his thoughtfulness.

After a few minutes, I said softly, "Please excuse me if I close my eyes for a minute."

"Oh, you are tired. You sleep. I will let you sleep," he replied as I closed my eyes, my headache gone and nausea subsiding.

Later, I was vaguely aware of our exiting the freeway, still a little groggy as we neared my street, amazed we were at my door so quickly.

As he pulled my bags from the trunk, he offered me some figs from one of his many fruit trees, and I resisted the urge to hug him, so thankful to be delivered home. I was lighter, cooler, enveloped in kindness and ready to curl in close to my husband.

Part II – *Life as a Parent*

Don't Spook the Teenager

(First published in Literary Mama, July/August 2022)

This seems like a typical Sunday evening. My husband and I are on the couch while our 14-year-old son works on homework upstairs. On other nights he might make an appearance on the landing to share a short anecdote with us before quickly returning to his room. This night, however, he descends the stairs, notebook in hand, and asks, "Dad, can you help me with this?"

My chest begins to constrict with labored breathing, my palms moistening. I am afraid any sudden movement or hint of rising enthusiasm will alarm my boy and cause him to retreat. It's like spotting majestic wildlife wandering in the Serengeti, animals who mildly acknowledge the human spectator as they forage for food . . .or in this case, come in search of homework assistance. The teenager has come in close to his parents. And I don't want to spook him.

Feigning nonchalance, I scoot over as he climbs in

between us eager to resolve his algebra dilemma. He stretches his long limbs out alongside me while leaning into his dad.

I can vaguely hear my husband's voice discussing percentages, kilograms, and solutions. "Ok, 500 times 60 percent equals how many liters?" But the warmth of my boy next to me drowns out any talk of equations as I relish this rare closeness. Like the muscle memory of riding a bike, I can feel the weight of him in our early years together when he spent afternoons on my lap while I read out loud.

He didn't have a security blanket or special stuffed animal as a child, just the comfort of twirling my hair as he sucked his thumb, his head tucked in under my chin. I grieved when this bonding abruptly ended after a visit to the dentist who had the audacity to encourage my four-year-old to stop sucking his thumb. This young kid then had the audacity to follow the dentist's instructions and stopped sucking his thumb that same day. When the thumb-sucking ended, twirling mom's hair soon ended as well. However, there were still moments when I would reach for him, and he would rest in my hug. Moments when he didn't stiffen.

"Mom! Dude!" he often now exclaims while pushing himself loose.

Sure, there are still occasional, fleeting moments when my boy, nearly matching my five feet nine inches, lets me kiss him on the cheek or share a quick embrace before school, but they are scarce, like getting up close to an armored pangolin on the plains of Tanzania.

My psychologist friend assures me this is a valuable

part of individuation for early teens.

She suggests we are creating a safe space for him to push boundaries and separate as he tries on independence. But I wrestle with a familiar paradox in parenting, celebration that he is becoming his own man and grief that his growing up means he will leave. Leave for friends, for college, for life. I don't want him to stay seven forever, but I also don't want him to leave.

My son shifts position so he is now mostly resting on me while he seeks to understand the last problems on the page.

"X is unknown, then you added to it?" my husband murmurs while my son attempts to explain his pencil scratch.

I am aware of the gentle voices going back and forth as they discuss the problems. No attitude. No guffaws or heavy sighs. Just a kid who needs help from his dad and feels safe enough to climb in between his parents and rest comfortably on his mom while he solves word problems.

". . .500 is the full quantity" my husband continues.

". . .so then 25 plus three zeros?" my son responds.

After writing a partial answer, my son, focused on his dad's words, casually adjusts his elbow onto my arm, an arm that freezes at my side, my breathing shallow so the rise and fall of my chest doesn't disrupt this connection. I don't follow the words they are saying, being so immersed in the deep maternal affection enveloping this space.

I am distracted from my reverie as my son asks with exasperation, "When am I going to use this anyway?"

Without thinking I exclaim,

"This is teaching you to think critically. To get your brain to look at problem solving in a particular way!"

I'm triumphant in my response before I clap my hands over my mouth, knowing this is not the moment for declarations about the importance of algebra. This is a moment for listening. For being still and being with. Perhaps a moment to stealthily record our time on the couch in the Notes section on my phone, channeling my nervous energy as I attempt to capture every last twitch and sigh next to me. His closeness is too precious to risk any premature departure. He is unguarded, unselfconscious here between us. A unique moment. A teenager with his defenses down.

My boy's feet gently move next to my leg. I am merely a cushion on the couch. *Don't fuck this up*, I think.

"X plus Y equals 100. But it's two different . . ." my husband is saying when my son interrupts.

"Okay, okay. I don't even understand this."

But frustration hasn't sent him back upstairs quite yet, although I sense this time together is almost done; when he has received enough help, he'll return to his cave.

My husband turns the paper over one more time to double-check a problem, pointing to the equation in question as my son nods.

And then, the work is done. He climbs off the couch.

"Thanks Dad."

"Love you," we both call after him, a little hitch in my voice as I turn to smile at my husband. I notice a glisten in his eyes as he smiles back.

She said, "You don't have a child with Down Syndrome."

When our first son was 18 months old, we decided it was time for a thaw. We had six frozen embryos and were ready to take them out of the freezer and try for a second child. A very technical process where, like chicken from a deep freeze, embryos are defrosted. Four were viable, cells dividing normally, and ready to be placed inside my uterus.

Yes. It's as romantic as it sounds.

Our doctor, fully aware of our parameters (we would not selectively reduce a fetus and we didn't want to be a TLC reality show: "Jud and Mandy Have Too Many"), implanted all four.

During our first round of in vitro fertilization in 2006, four embryos were implanted and I delivered one healthy baby boy. The doc's thinking here was based on my 20-plus years of endometriosis, and we were hopeful one embryo would stick around, maybe twins.

So, with this background, we held our breath and waited to see who might stay with us this second time.

This process is pretty straightforward and linear. We made this decision. The doc concurred. We moved ahead. But this is way too sterile.

Those of us who have walked the road of infertility know this intimately. My husband and I were the lucky ones, with two successful pregnancies after two IVF attempts. I am aware even typing that sentence, a woman or man reading this might be double-birding their copy of the book right now, the pain and longing from unsuccessful attempts uncontainable. It is all so grueling.

With our second round of IVF, we were reintroduced to the familiar protocol of daily injections of progesterone, gracefully given in one's ass. I was spared the days of stomach injections to stimulate eggs at my ovary doors. And I didn't miss the accompanying bruises that streaked across my abdomen.

We settled into the first trimester, as one does into a cozy couch (and by settling into a cozy couch, I mean pacing nightly with both nausea and anxiety while parenting an almost-two-year-old).

During our 13-week visit with our fertility doctor, she noticed a slight thickening in the back of the baby's neck and said, "You don't have a baby with Down Syndrome. But it would be good to see my perinatologist friend to take a look."

Um, what?

In all the decisions, practical and philosophical, that

accompany the choice to pursue IVF, we decided not to do genetic testing on the embryos. For many reasons. But at the time I didn't want to have to contemplate one more set of medical ethics questions. I didn't have the bandwidth. I also believed we were manipulating the system enough as it was. We wouldn't do so with this.

There was also the math. Eleven embryos total when we got started. Four implanted for our oldest. Four implanted for this pregnancy. One baby hanging on in there. We don't have a baby with Down Syndrome.

Here is where the pregnancy took a turn from nausea and anxiety to full-blown panic and fear.

After our first ultrasound with the specialist, she began her response by saying, "With all due respect to Dr. H..."
Shit.

And all the medical ethics questions I had tried to avoid came flooding in as we pivoted away from typical "What to Expect When You're Expecting" to "Are You Sure You Really Want to Have This Baby?"

It is important to pause for a minute and talk about denial and how my path diverged from my husband's. Our fear began to manifest itself in different ways and I was not open to his. We had to constantly interact with the messaging from genetic counselors that this was going to be a disaster. It wasn't explained in those words exactly, but when a list is handed to expecting parents of all the possible (what we interpreted as "likely") problems and complications that will befall the unborn baby, the word "disaster" seems fitting. Perhaps my biggest beef with this list was that it included "Leukemia" and omitted "Stubborn." That last one would have been a damn helpful inclusion.

And yes, leukemia is on the list. At that moment, I was deeply grateful one of my dearest childhood friends is a pediatric oncologist, who I called after this appointment in sheer panic. "How many patients with Down Syndrome have you had? What is the likelihood? How can I have the genetic counselor taken out and make it look like an accident?"

My wise friend gently said, "Let's meet this baby first and we'll go from there."

Ok.

With each appointment, we inched closer to the decision to get an amniocentesis, the test which can offer the most conclusive, but not 100% definitive, answer but also comes with the threat of miscarrying. My denial had me spinning with what-ifs while my husband quietly struggled with a desperate need to "just know." He never pressed. He kept much of his turmoil to himself but was hoping we could get the test and prepare ourselves for the actuality of the diagnosis, or at least get a little closer to certainty.

It is his story to tell, but there was an element of thinking that if this ended the pregnancy it wouldn't be all bad. There would be some relief. I understand that better now.

But, the baby was alive and kicking inside me. There was mama bear shit happening that would not even entertain that possibility. His fear was real. And so was mine.

We went with the amnio after a call to some close friends with a two-year-old son with Down Syndrome. Both were encouraging us to move forward with this, but her words were direct, "Do it. You will be glad you know."

She was right.

After the fluid was extracted and the doctor held it up, she knew almost conclusively by the color. Down Syndrome.

This was about week 20. We now had 20 more weeks to let this sink in. (Fourteen actually. He arrived early.)

And I confess those following weeks are a blur. I mentioned I had an almost two-year-old, a creative funny boy who was always in motion. I was and am so grateful for him, for the distraction, for the fun it was to bake with him and paint with him and read with him. We three got ready for this new baby brother.

Down Syndrome.

What I do know is that throughout that time I held out hope, or held onto denial. Nothing is 100% conclusive. I secretly listened for stories of false diagnoses. I combed the internet late at night. I began to collect stories of amazing people with Down Syndrome doing amazing things, beating the odds. Not having leukemia. It is a challenging juxtaposition to hold: Hope in what might not be and hope in what is.

In week 36, one month to the due date, my water broke at noon on a Saturday while watching TV with my husband. Our oldest was next door playing with our close friends when we called to say, "Um. I think we're having a baby today. Can he stay with you?" His first sleepover.

The details of the afternoon are rather benign. Basic labor, epidural, Pitocin to get contractions going, nurses telling us heartwarming stories about cousins, friends, siblings with Down Syndrome who are amazing. This was the gift we did not anticipate. Knowing beforehand that our child had Down Syndrome meant everyone who came into the room knew. And it encouraged them to dig around for their own heartwarming experiences to share while we waited.

But denial was still in the wings, there was still a lingering drop of hope that maybe we wouldn't have to start this journey.

This was stoked when our five-pound boy was delivered after one push (if I could order this delivery as Christmas gifts for friends I would) and the resident pediatrician came in for the initial checks. He looked. He checked. He left. No word about DS. We looked at each other.

Ten minutes later he returned and exclaimed to the room, "This baby has Down Syndrome." Our boy had faked out the pediatrician! There were no significant markers, no palmar crease, no pronounced eyes, except for the regular distortions that occur with swelling.

We didn't realize we were holding our breath until the actual actuality set in.

Our boy was here. He was exquisitely small and beautiful, all the clichés. He was healthy.

He had Down Syndrome.

That is not the end of the story. We are 13 years in now and I am beginning to dig into the corners of my mind where I have stored the harder, unexamined parts of life with Down Syndrome. I am afraid to go back there, with the dust and cobwebs. But even if I avoid those places, they still exist, and not only in my mind but in a larger cultural conversation, as evidenced in a 2020 article in *The*

Atlantic.

The medical ethics questions haven't retreated, rather they reemerge from time to time when I least expect them; when I'm going about the day-to-day.

So, this is a start. A way of pulling out the boxes of ideas and feelings I have tucked away under the stairs. The conclusion here a beginning.

Living in the Extra

(First published on scarymommy.com)

Recently, I was checking my email and saw a message with exciting personal news. I yelled out with enthusiasm. My youngest, who has Down Syndrome, jumped up from his seat at the computer with screams of his own. He didn't know what we were celebrating. But if there is celebrating in our house, then he is in!

It isn't just celebrating.

It's *extra* celebrating.

Having a birthday? He is right there to light the candles and sing.

At 6 am.

When my husband arrives home from a 24-hour shift at the fire station, my boy is cheering throughout the house, "Dad's home! Mom, Dad is home."

Hell. If I've just returned from the grocery store, he is not just jazzed about my arrival, he is forcefully rallying the troops (his older brother) to help empty the car. "G!

Mom's back!"

Life with a child with Down Syndrome is *extra*.

This extra isn't just in celebrating, which is a delightful manifestation. This also plays out in other ways. Starting with his chromosomes. (He has an extra copy of chromosome number 21.) There are even extra words typed in the sentence to express people-first language, "person with Down Syndrome."

Our three-step nightly routine of Bath, Bed, Book is extended to thirty-five steps, which include a thousand prompts and multiple reminders such as, "No, you need to sleep in your bed, not ours."

Extra also looks like extra waiting to reach certain childhood milestones: crawling; walking; talking; going to the bathroom alone.

And friends often say this is just like typical kids. Typical strong-willed kids, for instance.

Yes. There are some typical aspects. But sometimes there aren't.

I imagine friends offer examples of sameness to build a bridge and create some sense of solidarity because the differences are so obvious. Oh, you have a strong-willed child? So, do I.

But so often I have craved the verbal acknowledgment of the differences, the uniqueness in parenting my boy. In the last few years, I've begun to realize that the people around me *do* see the differences and I might be the one with a few blind spots; having closed off from just how challenging all this can be.

Parenting a child with Down Syndrome isn't just living

in the *extra*, it is also holding tension in paradoxes. My son is like typical kids and different than typical kids. Both are true. A paradox.

These paradoxes, with all their tension and complexity, often fuel my desire to bury any discussion about Down Syndrome and simply get on with life. But, conversely, I also want to talk about all the complexities, the differences, all the *extra*, even when I can't always articulate it very well.

This can be a tall order.

It is all quite confusing for me because I see the Down Syndrome diagnosis all the time and I don't see it at all.

Another paradox. The former is because it's quite obvious. He has the familiar look of Down Syndrome. The latter may be a mixture of some denial and blind spots I mentioned before with a lot of "just going about our days."

Having a child who falls outside of, or below, neurotypical standards certainly has its challenges.

Some of these challenges are specific to Down Syndrome and some are specific to parenting a human. There have been many ways in which I wanted to start this story, with anecdotes and examples but often it is hard to clearly explain what makes these moments unique to Down Syndrome.

This can all be quite jumbled in my head.

It is also critical to note, the *extra* in parenting a child with Down Syndrome is different for every single family.

Similar to the Autism spectrum, there is a Down Syndrome spectrum that includes many variations and abilities in categories like cognitive functioning, speech development, muscle tone, health and dual diagnoses.

Understanding this continuum is critical to understanding Down Syndrome. We families are all in the same club, waving the Down Syndrome flag, but our day-to-day experiences are very different. There is solidarity in the similarities and value in being aware of the differences. I even intentionally use "I" language when talking about this because my experience is distinct from my husband's.

My child with Down Syndrome sits on a high-functioning end of the spectrum I mentioned above. For example, he has high muscle tone, is athletic with strong hand-eye coordination (from his mother), and had an early aptitude with a straw, which apparently was a thing.

He reads, often out loud to himself on his bed, usually "Diary of a Wimpy Kid." But he is uninterested in retelling the details of the story. We don't know if this is because of limited comprehension, difficulty in speech or articulation or if he's a twelve-year-old boy who simply doesn't want to talk about it.

So, we are in the club, we have the membership, but each member is distinct.

Back to *extra*.

When my husband and I embrace in a hug, and our youngest observes this, he can be heard uttering a variation of, "Oh we're doing this?" as he drags a stool across the floor, then wiggles his way in between us. Sometimes, he wraps his arms around us as he calls to his brother, insisting he come down for a Ream Team hug.

And if his mind is set on this course, he does not relent

until all four Reams are standing in an embrace.

It is best just to comply. And, why wouldn't we?

Well, sometimes we don't want to continue our group hug because love and affection are great but so is space.

And sometimes, we need space. (Connection and autonomy. Another paradox.) It is a dance between these two experiences. It feels shitty to rebuff a child with Down Syndrome his affection. But if that affection has been offered twenty times already in one morning, it can feel suffocating.

Sometimes it is our boy who wants the space. When he was very little, walking but not speaking, he would simply leave. Quietly slip out the door and elope (a new connotation of this word for us. He wasn't getting married. He was leaving.) His mind set on exploration and discovery. It wasn't until kind neighbors knocked on our door that our horror would take over as we realized Chas wasn't in the house. His eloping was extra.

My son is happy and content, a stereotype of Down Syndrome. Except for the times when he isn't.

This is usually when he is asked to shift into a "non-preferred activity." I also don't like to do "non-preferred" activities because they are, well, non-preferred. It's in the name. So, in that way he is typical.

However, his non-compliance (another great term we have learned on this journey that means he won't do what we want him to do), is extra. It's Olympic.

And we are the coaches forming and shaping his behavior so he will be healthy and clean.

And sometimes these coaches drink.

These vignettes offer both a glimpse into our experience while also illustrating the challenging nature of it all, the contradictions and complexities. In many ways, this is all just parenting. But it is *extra* parenting.

For some of us in this club, the extra itself is extra. The expected speech delays are more delayed or speech never comes. The delayed potty-training extends well beyond the toddler years into adolescence. Learning can also be slow, the pace extra slow, with extra patience required.

As I type, my boy is upstairs playing on his iPad. This is not a quiet activity. He is yelling at the screen, talking to the characters. When he is finished, he will probably come downstairs, transitioning to his next activity.

And with each transition, he will declare, "Mom. I love you."

This sentence is definitive.

Insistent.

Important.

This is a statement shared with me multiple times a day.

Not said, declared. "Mom. I love you." All day.

He doesn't just love. He loves *extra*.

Watching From the Pier

He is down there, in rolling water, waiting in a radiant streak of sunlight, sitting casually as if he was resting on our living room couch and not straddling a board nine hundred feet from shore, unknown mysteries trolling beneath his feet. I wanted this for him even when he was still growing inside me as I swam in the warm Atlantic and the cold Pacific. A child who loves the water. But I didn't know it would look like this, at home in the untamed ocean, his habitat, like a dolphin playing in waves.

In one swift movement, with deceptive ease, he is standing. No, he is dancing, miraculously. A miracle to the watching mother who tried this once, enjoyed the paddle but wondered, baffled, at how a body can go so quickly from prostrate to vertical.

Behind me a toddler runs along the boards, his parents calling after him. A smile across his face. Laughter. And suddenly I see my boy, age two, running along this same stretch of concrete and wood, me following close behind.

I turn away from this memory with the incredulity of a parent continuously stunned by the passing of time, time that moves along without empathy. I can feel time in my bones, its speed, its indiscriminate way of aging everything, without negotiating or placating, without pause. I will sit for another hour and marvel at my boy's independence growing exponentially before my eyes.

A man-child in the water becoming one of the iconic surfers.

My boy, silhouetted against the bright sun, is a sleek black form like the others who wait beside him, only recognizable by a distinctive flip of wet hair, the bobbing of his head in sync with his arms as he moves through the water.

Sometimes his shape is indecipherable in the blinding shimmer.

He studies the approaching waves as they arrive in smooth, glassy sets. January water. No wind to fluster the surface with white caps that would impede the view to the horizon. A view perfect for scanning, looking for water spouts, the humpback whales migrating south to Mexico for the winter. My attention is divided between my boy and the possibility of seeing these majestic creatures at home in this water, like my son, free to move without constraint.

It seems the surfable waves are few and far between today, often only discernible by the deep rumbling that moves through the pod of surfers, like lowing cattle, who call out to one another a set is coming in.

Get it. Get it. Get it.

I am not alone. This is a popular attraction. People gather along the rail and watch the surfers, like seeing penguins at the zoo. But unlike the birds trapped in an enclosure, the riders below are free. My boy is free, not restrained by a box; a mother's fantasy, that he could be kept safe behind glass.

There are no boundaries in this water. There is danger on that board. There is risk. But with the risk there is great beauty. The sun on the water, a beam of light stretching over the dark waves. Each ripple flashes, like fireworks being thrown across the surface. In this magically illuminated gleam my son waits in the throng of other seekers for his next ride.

Does my boy comprehend how magnificent it is to have such freedom in this water? Can he see the beauty? Does he understand this at fourteen? Perhaps. For there is something that pulls him out of bed before sunrise to ride silently on his bike to the sand, his board ready at his side, when others his age still sleep. A voice calls to him in the darkness.

I glimpse my boy in the shadow of the pier as he paddles out after a long run pumping his board nearly to shore, here in his home swell that hosts thousands.

I watch to cement memories that will come to me later when I am not sitting on a cold stone bench with my feet resting on the rails, my forehead leaning against the smooth upper bar, with permission to watch my boy, at a distance.

I watch to remember that when he is here in the water, he is alive. He is free.

We Have a Snake

I have a very strange relationship with a snake. This dawned on me one morning while I was whispering to the one in my son's room through a mesh screen as it moved towards the top of its cage.

When I watch this creature, I often wonder, what was I so afraid of?

This relationship has developed slowly, but consistently, during my daily visits to make sure it is still in its cage after it escaped just one month into its arrival at our home. The escaping is what I had initially been afraid of.

We have this snake because I am certifiably, objectively, the best mom in the world.

For years, I would rebuff my son's request for a snake with a very simple and direct message. "Hell. No."

My emphatic certainty was fueled by the stories of every single person I've ever known with a snake about how their snake escaped into hidden spaces in their homes. Some never to be found again.

Every. Single. Person.

I was insistent. "I will never soften! I will never change my mind!" And if I ever did (and here, reader, is the little chink in my armor – the "if"), I would reserve the right to stay at the local five-star hotel if we ever had a snake-escape story of our own.

Then I had a hysterectomy.

And of course, you see the natural connection here.

This surgery had been recommended to me for a long time. I needed it and I was afraid, irrationally or otherwise, about hitting menopause in such an abrupt way. I was afraid of how my body would respond and the additional hormonal challenges I would face.

This was the culmination of years of battling severe endometriosis and managing it with multiple surgeries.

I was tired and anxious about it.

Although my body had been suffering pain for a long time, I did not want another surgery. My fear and anxiety kept me from the relief it would bring.

I had the surgery.

As I rested in bed after the procedure, I began to reflect on my fears, specific to this circumstance and more broadly existential, asking, "What had I been afraid of? What role had fear played in this whole process? How might I use this experience to move towards my fears in the future?"

Perhaps you can already see where this is going.

While I waxed philosophic, my son came in to visit me and to ask yet again if he could have a snake. But this time he added, "Mom, what are you so afraid of?" Timing is everything.

Tenacity and timing.

For a brief moment of elation, or post-surgical delirium, I thought, "What *am* I afraid of?"

And I said yes.

Perhaps this is a story about facing fears. But this is certainly *not* a story about why you should get a snake.

Maybe it's a story about facing fears within the confines of clear boundaries, or in my case, firm secure lift-proof terrarium lids.

Because I faced my fears, I agreed to this pet. And this pet escaped.

A few weeks into snake ownership, my sons and I went to pick up my mom from the airport. Both boys were excited to show off our newest addition to the family. It was late when we arrived home. My husband was at the fire station and I was eager to get through the bedtime routine and into bed.

We funneled into my son's room with great anticipation to discover an empty cage. No snake.

And all my threats of heading to the local hotel faded into the ether as I surprisingly moved into problem-solving mode.

I was less afraid than I thought I would be. Sure, I threw up in my mouth a little and didn't sleep very well that night after some futile searching. But I stayed in the house for those two days.

Two days!

I comforted my son and strategized how to locate the missing snake.

I put a live mouse in an open cage in the middle of my son's room to entice the thing out of hiding to eat.

I tried not to make eye-contact with the rodent anytime I came near that room. I felt ashamed but focused.

We put small bowls of water around the house to coax it into the open. And then one night, I decided to roam the dark house with my flashlight to see if this being was nocturnal.

It was.

As I stood in the hallway outside my bedroom door, between my room and the guest room where my mom slept, this small corn snake slithered from my room and paused before heading into hers. This is when I learned my son sleeps like the dead.

He could not be roused. No amount of shaking or pleading would wake him and I quickly realized I would have to capture this thing on my own. Well, me and my mother. (My husband was once again at the fire station. This is also not a "breaking down gender role stereotypes" story.)

When my mom heard me rustling in the hallway outside her open door, her eyes suddenly opened.

"Did you find it?"

"Yes."

As I yelled to her, "Get the cage, get the cage," I reached for a handy wooden back scratcher and together we wrangled Scales (we are creative name givers in our home) back into its cage.

I sure as hell wasn't going to touch it.

My mother is a delightful woman not prone to great bursts of enthusiasm like I am. She celebrates in quieter ways. But not when she has just successfully captured her first rogue snake late at night in her daughter's house!

We danced and jumped and yelled at our victory.

My boys slept on.

That was five years ago.

Every day I check on Scales, making sure she (as decided by my oldest) is still there. Until we upgraded the terrarium, there was a large collection of heavy objects stacked on the lid for safe measure, ensuring no escape route, no loose edge.

Over time, however, my daily checks have the slightest traces of tenderness, if not affection.

I still don't want to touch or hold her, but I make sure she has enough water. I am often in charge of purchasing the live feed for her. On a rare occasion, I will actually feed her if I'm the only one home.

And every so often, I chuckle at my fears. Yes, I have made sure every risk is accounted for here. I don't want her to be my bedfellow anytime soon. But sometimes I find myself whispering to this animal while marveling at the absolutes I put forth, my proclamations of never.

A final note.

Recently, I was cleaning out under my bed, taking advantage of the switch we were making to a new mattress.

It's amazing what can collect under a bed over twenty years. As I dusted and vacuumed, I noticed some animal droppings both on the floor and tucked into the box springs. It wasn't rat scat. (I've been studying that in my garage.)

What could it be?

There wasn't a lot of it.

A mystery.

And then it dawned on me as it has most likely just dawned on you.

This might be a story about examining our fears, but I want to reiterate, this is *not* a story encouraging people to buy snakes.

The Ordinary

What is a group of fourteen-year-old boys? A gaggle? A posse? I am wondering this as I watch five of them leave my driveway on electric bikes cruising down the street, fishing poles in hand. Heading to an age-old pastime on a modern convenience.

I am trying to identify the flutter in my heart as they arrive and leave, their entire time in my garage mere minutes. They don't stage here very often and I love to see my son in his element with his people, to listen to the comments they make, the casual, direct conversations they have about baseball, or friends, or what supplies they'll need for fishing.

One boy knocks on the door and although I have known him since elementary school, I don't recognize the man-child on the doorstep. His face more resembles his dad and older brother and less the cherubic towhead he once was. His voice is deeper too.

"How are you doing, Mason?" I ask.

"Great. How are you?" he responds in a deep voice that is almost comical, how far it is from the little boy voice I remember.

More kids arrive. They are cordial and even engaging, greeting the little brother and me standing in the garage, pretending to have something to do but just wanting to be in their orbit for a minute. They are bright-eyed, joking with one another. Comfortable in their own skin, enjoying the freedom of being fourteen on a Monday afternoon with the last days of eighth grade just weeks away.

Summer is so close they can taste it. Fishing is a forecasting of what summer will hold when they aren't at baseball camp or surfing or on trips with their families.

Watching the boys leave the driveway, calling to one another as they head down the street and towards the beach, I am struck by the silly analogy at play. Their leaving is a hallmark of their independence. The launching. I want my son to do this over and over again with good people. But watching the boys turn the corner at the end of the street, I feel a hitch in my throat.

I return to my chores and attend to my younger son. Head to the grocery store and start dinner. But I am profoundly thankful I paused to capture this little snapshot of my fourteen-year-old boy with his friends on a regular Monday afternoon.

I remind myself often that I don't want my boy to stay a boy forever and there is grief at each parenting chapter as it closes, which makes a moment like this special.

I witnessed something sacred in the mundane today.

I am thankful I was paying attention enough to notice.

Part III – *Life In My Head*

I don't want to. I just don't.

Today, I don't want to move toward a goal, go ahead with the plan, meet a need, fulfill a desire, or cross things off my list.

I don't want to scroll through Instagram, check email, or answer texts. I don't want to make plans, meet for lunch, or talk on the phone.

I don't want to be productive. I don't want to be unproductive. I don't want to feel guilty or ashamed or useless for playing the stupidest of games on my phone where the only goal is to fill in the gaps until lines disintegrate.

I don't want to get off the couch.

I don't want to be vulnerable or examine my inner world or explore my feelings or understand why I'm in this place right now. I don't want to push through or just do it or snap out of it or wash my face or be untamed.

I don't want to be the bigger person. I don't want to be the lesser person. I don't want to be on a journey or in process. I don't want to be human?

I don't want to eat vegetables or drink water or monitor calories or count steps. I don't want to feel bad about drowning this day in complex carbohydrates.

I don't want my knees to hurt.

I don't want to go for a walk or practice meditation or start a gratitude journal or stand with my bare feet in the grass or call a friend. I don't want to read my book or fold laundry or get rid of the ant colony that has taken up residence in my kitchen. I don't want to sweep away the dog hair from where it is blanketing the wood floors.

I don't want to be in this funk.

I don't want to feel this lousy about my face or my ass or my hair or my teeth. I don't want to worry about bathing suit season or being liked or what other people think of me. I don't want to feel like I've wasted time worrying about all of these things.

I don't want to fear death or wonder if there's a God or feel grief. I don't want to have anxiety or worry about catastrophic events or speculate if there will be enough water for my grandchildren. I don't want to worry about gas prices or inflation rate hikes or that there might be another rattlesnake under a paddleboard when we go camping next summer.

I don't want everyone to be so on edge.

I don't want to be so on edge.

I don't want to be this judgmental, this irritated, or this hypocritical.

I don't want to be seen. I don't want to be unseen. I don't want to be known. I don't want to be unknown. I don't want this rollercoaster of highs and lows.

I don't want to see life as so complicated, so confusing, so complex, or so gray but I don't want to think in black and white.

I don't want to live in so many paradoxes.

I don't want to add any whimsy to this, even though I wish there was some whimsy to add.

I don't want to forget the weight of my husband's hand on my hip as we fall asleep.

When the Need to Be In Water is Threatened by Body Issues

(First published in Menopause: Life Lessons & Memories)

I love being in water.

Fully submerged, swimming in it, frolicking like a young child. Especially cold water; the kind of cold that immediately heightens all the senses, elevates the heart rate, causing an undeniable awareness of being alive.

I have been known to yell those exact words, "I'm alive!" Frankenstein-like as I walk from the waves after a long swim in the ocean. This is sometimes greeted with everything from utter amazement to sheer bafflement to near horror as some of my friends watch in disbelief. "How can you do that?!"

I'm invigorated. Energized. Alive!

I'm not picky. Cold water is my favorite but I'm open to tepid water if the air is cooler. I even enjoy a hot tub with its 104-degree temps from time to time. If I can be in water, all is right in my world for those moments. My outlook on life improves; my senses awaken; my soul healed.

It isn't just that the water itself is marvelous.

There are wonders to be found in water.

I remember one particularly therapeutic swim off the coast of Santa Barbara just a few miles from the small college I attended. On that day, I took a few deep breaths before plunging into the frigid water and swimming to the buoys that line the coast.

After reaching one buoy, I turned around to swim back and noticed a large, sleek object just feet from where I tread; a dolphin was swimming between me and my destination. I froze, awe-struck and afraid, so close to something so wild.

If there is a pool, river, lake, or ocean nearby and I have a bathing suit, I am pulled to that water like a magnetic power.

But sometimes, there is a greater force that keeps me from accessing what I know is undeniably life-giving.

Despite the deep goodness I experience being in water, I am not always able to get into the water with ease, even if it is nearby. This is, in large part, because being in water usually involves putting my body in a bathing suit. And I've been at war with this body for a very long time.

My earliest memories of hating this body start midway through elementary school, age nine. As I sat in a bath one night critically evaluating my thighs, I stretched the skin around my upper legs, attempting to fold it under me. I wanted to make them look thinner, imagining what it might be like to just cut off the "extra" parts.

A few years later I was at a sleepover with friends, seventh grade, and we were giving each other nicknames. At least, I believe everyone was getting nicknames, but I can only remember mine. Where the general details are fuzzy, my nickname is not. Thunder Thighs. Then we all toasted. All I can hear is a loud cheer, "To Thunder Thighs." My voice included.

That was 35 years ago.

I look back at pictures of myself at these ages. Big smiles and bad haircuts. Awkward clothes and gaps where teeth didn't grow in. But in all of these images, I see a body that was fairly unremarkable in its size. Average for whatever average is. But the lies were creeping in.

In my teen years and early adult life, I began to shift my weight up and down, enjoying the comfort and full-stomach sensations that came from eating before deciding to lose weight when the enjoying got away from me; gaining and losing the same 20 pounds a number times over the next 20 years.

Reviewing old photos of myself creates a palpable tension because in looking back I often like what I see. A bright young 20-something. A smiling 30-year-old woman. A laughing mother in her 40s.

But I also know that in the moments those pictures were taken, I was generally consumed with self-loathing, utterly distracted by oppressive opinions about how I looked, or how fat I perceived myself to be.

The tension is also laced with shame at not being grateful enough for the healthy body in the pictures. These ideas persist today.

Now, when I'm getting my picture taken, knowing that I continue to detest this body, I often wonder if I will look back at this moment and think, "Oh, my shape was just fine, my skin clear, my eyes bright. Oh, I wasn't so loathsome."

Perhaps I'll look back at the photos of today, much like I do of the ones from the past, and remember the setting, the people, the experience, and *not* how my pants fit or how my chin looked.

I often wonder what my 75-year-old self would tell 48-year-old me in these pictures. It is baffling to see this whole toxic system so clearly, but feel unable to bypass it in order to embrace this body right now.

There's been enough destructive energy heaped onto these thighs, how does one get free? I am still working on this.

Sometimes I ask myself, "Am I just extra susceptible to the cultural messages that constantly swirl around me, the images and ideas that I should look a certain way? Be a certain size?" Sometimes I sit with friends and as the conversation continues around me, I wonder if I'm alone in wanting to throw in the towel, get off the hamster wheel, stop talking about weight and just live.

I'm exhausted from the constant barrage, the never-silent loudspeaker, that yells, "You are not okay. You cannot be okay in that body!" You must "fix, shape, smooth, shrink."

This constant barrage requires constant vigilance.

Some days I have the energy to keep this tidal wave

offshore. And other days I don't.

In all of this, I know there is one lifeline that will serve as a balm for these wounds, a calm when I'm caught in all this tumult. But the crazy thing is, it requires me to put on a bathing suit.

Regardless of how badly I feel in my skin. No matter how demeaning I am to my body, this body still needs to be in water.

In her book, "Traveling Mercies: Some Thoughts on Faith," author Anne Lamott writes about heading to the beach during a vacation in Mexico:

> *"I was not wearing a cover-up, not even a T-shirt. I had decided I was going to take my thighs and butt with me proudly wherever I went. I decided, in fact, on the way to the beach that I would treat them as if they were beloved elderly aunties, the kind who did embarrassing things at the beach, like roll their stockings into tubes around their ankles, but who I was proud of because they were so great in every real and important way. So we walked along, the three of us, the aunties and I, to meet Sam and our friends in the sand. I imagined that I could feel the aunties beaming, as if they had been held captive in a dark closet too long, like Patty Hearst. Freed finally to stroll on a sandy Mexican beach: what a beautiful story. It did not trouble me that parts of my body — the auntie parts — kept moving even after I had come to a full halt. Who cares? People just need to be soft and clean."*

Wisdom from a wise woman, Mama Anne.

On first reading this I realized her thighs were not named Thunder. They were welcomed as cherished members of the family. I cling to this magnanimous view of one's body as I try to be grateful for the legs that can walk me into the water.

There were years when I didn't let myself swim, the walk into the water from my chair or towel too mortifying, too vulnerable to overcome. I was cemented to the ground unable to get to what I knew was goodness in a pure form.

Sometimes, I would sit demurring when a friend beckoned me to the waves. "No thanks. I don't want to swim."

For me to say no thank you to swimming is like saying, "No thank you. I don't want to breathe air." It doesn't make sense. But I let the weight (pun intended) weigh me down on the sand or pool chair.

Sure, there were times when the voices of self-loathing didn't always win. They don't always win now. It just requires a seemingly super-human power to turn away from all the messages that declare this body unfit for the public.

I pull Anne Lamott's words out like an energy drink, to give me the strength to walk these thighs in all their bare glory across the sand or past the pool chairs.

As I've gotten older, life has gotten harder, more complicated, in many ways, with all that adulting requires. And the all-encompassing necessity of swimming has become even clearer. It is an unfailing reprieve. I am certain that if I can get in water, I can experience some relief.

Sometimes, though, trying to get to the water is like a snail crawl through quicksand. I give power to the voices that remind me I'm not "beach body ready," which is regularly reinforced because I live in a Southern California beach city.

When I succumb to that messaging, I am denied access to one sure thing that will restore my soul. Some seasons I'm more successful than others.

Last year, I started meeting with a small group of women who get together to advise, encourage, and celebrate one another. I started meeting with the group at a particularly low point in my spirit, where I was acutely aware that there were good things available, life-giving tools, but I couldn't reach them. I was paralyzed by the oppressive inner voices.

I was believing everything the voices were saying. I was not getting in water very often.

During one Friday gathering, we each declared our goals for the coming month. I said, "I will go to the ocean regularly each week and put my feet in the water." One of my friends immediately responded, "I think you should put your whole body in that water every week. A couple of times a week, in fact."

She had heard me talk about how therapeutic water is for me and was trying to help me bypass the destructive internal lies that were keeping me from a really good thing.

So, I modified my goal.

I committed to putting this body in a bathing suit every few days and getting in the ocean.

This was particularly noteworthy because I am on the other side of menopause and my journey through a hysterectomy and beyond has left me with some additional padding. Padding I have really wanted to hide.

But I put my bathing suit on anyway.

You might see me. I am the middle-aged woman swimming and frolicking out in the waves like a young child at the beach for the first time. It is pure and uncontaminated joy in its purest form.

The voices in my head have been loudly condemning the body I'm in for so long but I continue to slowly dismantle their power.

With practice and intention, I can sometimes overcome the messages and get to the water. Sometimes I need close friends in my corner, friends who know me and can direct me with louder voices than the ones in my head. My friends shout, "Get to the water! And get in!"

So, despite the ongoing work I still need to do here, I put my bathing suit on anyway.

The Shoulds Are Taking Over

I find myself with a little extra space and quiet today. Space and quiet that I long for when I don't have it. But, I often fear the space I desperately want because when I have this openness in my time and my mind... the Shoulds take over.

I have long used the phrase "don't should on yourself" borrowed from an unremembered source but so clearly articulating a familiar feeling. What I should be doing.

In adulting, there are many necessary Shoulds. I should brush my teeth daily. I should sleep regularly. I should include water in my diet. I should pay the electricity bill to have power. Reasonable.

But there are Shoulds that whisper scathingly into my ears, that creep around my mind in ways that make me want to retreat to the couch and stream hours of television shows. The ideas themselves aren't necessarily bad but it's the intonation of the should, the sneering, the judgment. You should use this time to write, to exercise, to eat a vegetable. All good things.

But I can't access the good because I feel I've failed before I begin.

So, I eat iced Christmas cookies I made with my son.

I have long tried to understand this paralysis, this avoidance. I have acquired so many tools for successful living but there is always a sheen of "do more," "be more." My inability to measure what is enough panics me. Debilitates me.

I am unfamiliar with resting in "good enough." There is resignation, a mediocrity in it, and mediocre feels like the ultimate sin. I can see that some of this could read like "confessions of a perfectionist." But I often declare, I'm not a perfectionist, because I'm not, well, perfect. I am simply not good enough to be a perfectionist. This word conjures myopic focus, discipline, and drive, *not* re-watching Gilmore Girls as a soothing balm for anxiety.

More Christmas cookies.

I write this for two reasons, to explore the anxiety I feel as I type these words, and to share descriptions of an experience I think might be familiar to others. It is an isolating feeling, the crushing sensation of compounding Shoulds.

With that sentence comes an arrow, from the back of my mind to my chest, causing a geyser of anxiety like Old Faithful. The sensation accompanies a vision of a woman standing above me, arms crossed, rolling her eyes in contempt as she says, "Really? You pathetic, navel-gazing comfortable middle-class whiner. Why should you have feelings or needs or angst?"

Of course, she is me.

And she is very unkind.

Perhaps the biggest Should is that I must stay in motion when I want to sit. That I have space means I should fill it. And not just with anything. I should fill it well. With sit-ups or a chapter in a heady text about cultural analysis or chores. Apparently, the toilets aren't going to clean themselves.

Perhaps this is all insipid and vapid and easily cured with all the things people post about on social media, all the Shoulds that they accomplish.

But, I am beaten down by all the Shoulds.

Right now, there is one Should calling for attention. I can hear it faintly in the distance. It gently suggests I should take a look at all of this. Examine it. Ask, what is this about?

Perhaps I should even share it. There is often compassion in sharing.

Depression Isn't Fair

"Depression takes all my vibrant colors and bashes them together until I am gray, gray, gray... Perhaps this is why so many depressed people become artists, to reclaim the power of answering the question: What is the point? We are clawing at the ground with pen and paper while drowning in quicksand."

Glennon Doyle, "Untamed".

"What's the point?" That's my prevailing thought on this bright sunny day in Southern California. I want the sky to match what I feel inside. Instead, I wrestle with the profound incongruity between what is external and what is internal.

The sun is mocking me.

I fear writing that question, "What's the point?" It is something I ask more often than I want to admit because there is often an accompanying flood of insufficient answers that come back at me. The point is...

These words don't just come back at me, they are yelled at me, THE POINT IS...!!! The answers try to pull me out of the hole.

But this depression is not an intellectual exercise of trying to answer that question. It is an experiential questioning with existential-crisis undertones.

Right now, I am dressed to get good things, such as a dose of Vitamin D at my nearby beach. Yet I am overwhelmed by the extraordinary effort required to put one foot in front of the other to go get something I think will be life-giving.

It also takes so much effort to turn away from things that will end up heaping shame onto the darkness, things like french fries that so fleetingly numb but don't bring any light to the dark spaces.

Then my mind plays tricks on me.

I imagine all the people I know who aren't depressed, who wake up to another beautiful day on a holiday weekend and declare, "Yes! I am alive and ready to move into good things."

I want to declare that. I want to feel that. I want to feel that after I choose all the "right things" like eating my oatmeal with carefully curated toppings and turning off the news before it crushes me and putting on clothes that indicate to my body I am planning to go outside.

There are moments when I do feel the goodness of being awake and alive.

This isn't one of them.

The prevailing temptation in my body is to fold into a ball in the corner of a room and let Netflix wash over me until the feelings have passed.

But they are not passing. It has been a few days now and I move my feet like they are encased in cement shoes, trying to bypass the emotional heaviness and let my brain direct my steps.

Eat this for energy. Avoid the drive-thru because your body will rebel. Fold the laundry, order is helpful. Write some words, even if nothing is shared publicly. Avoid Instagram so you don't hate yourself and other people.

My brain is sending these signals like a lighthouse on a stormy day and I am out in turbulent waves, fighting to get to shore, dreaming of calmer waters.

But the flash storm seems to be only over my boat. I look across and others are enjoying placid seas.

Like a petulant child, I stomp my feet and say in my best Veruca Salt voice, "I want a calm and content inner world and I want it NOOOWWW!"

Then, I remember I am not alone. As I listen to NPR stories about the rising levels of depression, I realize others are in this fight as well. I think of my students, the college demographic, with high numbers in these areas.

I wonder, how do we take comfort in the awareness that others feel like we do? What compassion might I offer a fellow human stuck in a dark space? Can I extend that compassion to myself?

I'm not sure.

One balm does soothe. Writing.

Writing this down gets it out of my body. Rereading coherent sentences gives structure to what feels chaotic. Relieves the pressure.

I am not carrying it all in my bones. I'll let the words on the page hold some of the weight I carried in my chest.

And now, a bit of the cement has chipped off my feet and they are not as heavy to lift.

Some of the water has started to calm and my pitching boat is rocking a little more gently.

The sunshine is a bit more inviting than mocking. I may even go outside and take some of it in.

There is a little reprieve.

Part IV – *Life is a Journey*

Fine, Life's a Journey

I've been fighting it for many years now. It is a difficult point to concede, release, and accept. For so long, I have wanted to *arrive* in life, to be done with the journey. Then, and only then, I believed, life would truly begin.

I imagine you might be shaking your head at this naivety, this juvenile fantasy. But I have been clinging to the idea that at some point, like on a major milestone birthday, I would have solved all my problems, fixed all my issues, and life would continue on in a sea of total contentment, like joyfully playing a harp on a cloud of marshmallows.

Recently it hit me that if I'm joyfully playing a harp on a cloud of marshmallows...I am dead. (This is a loose illustration of what I think about the afterlife, but you get the point.)

I am not entirely sure how this idea became so ingrained in my mind and soul, but it is closely tied to my inability to accept myself as human and that the human condition means we are in process in perpetuity. I am not a fan of either, being a human or being in process. But whether or not I like this reality, I am learning it is, in fact, the way things are.

Life is a journey.

Last year, in order to further drill this idea into my head, I printed two photos of paths I'd taken in Oxford, England, and Poipu, Kawaii. I hung these prints in a prominent place in my dining room where I would see them every day and be reminded that I am on the path of life and the end is unknown, just like the paths in the pictures. And they are helping. Sort of. It appears I still need some convincing.

In a December 2022 interview with Allure Magazine, Jennifer Aniston talks about her own understanding of life as a journey. "I've realized you will always be working on stuff," she says. "I am a constant work in progress. Thank God. How uninteresting would life be if we all achieved enlightenment and that was it?"

For much of the last twenty years, I would have said I would be quite open, actually, to an uninteresting life in total enlightenment with everyone else.

The journey is exhausting.

Part of this is fueled by the feeling that I am alone in my struggles. Even when I intellectually know that other people are struggling right along with me, even people like Jennifer Aniston, I am so easily susceptible to believing they aren't.

This is why social media, for example, is tricky. I believe the images of smiling face after smiling face on a friend's page represent exactly how they are. They are this happy all the time. A part of my inner world actually believes this.

I remember a few years ago scrolling through my posts on Facebook trying to find a particular picture and stopping in alarm. I am just not this happy, I thought. Each picture was of me smiling. And we know that this is what we do with social media, present a curated package of ourselves. We know this. And we, at least I, very quickly forget it.

Because a part of me is so eager to be done with the journey, I am easily swayed into believing other people have achieved Nirvana, as evidenced by their social media pages, or are pretty darn close, and I too will get there soon.

This reminds me of a new podcast started by my close friend, a clinical psychologist. It is wisely titled "I Thought I Was Over This." A title so profound sometimes I just repeat it to myself without even listening to an episode.

I thought I was over this. I thought I was over this. I thought I was over this.

Dr. Kimber offers incredible permission to be human and to make mistakes. She normalizes the process of going back over and reexamining parts of ourselves we thought were healed, or complete, when in fact they are still a little out of whack or broken. (It is profoundly helpful to have friends in one's life that remind us it's okay to be human in all its complicated parts. It's additionally helpful when they start podcasts like this.)

So, then, what is the benefit of realizing life is a journey, that life doesn't hold one big destination of completeness (at least this side of death)? First, it's accepting reality. The truth is that being human is struggling, learning, growing, changing, and shaping. Again, I know this. But, I (we, for I now know I'm not alone) have difficulty accepting this sometimes.

Brene Brown acknowledges this in many conversations with her sisters on their podcast "Unlocking Us" as they discuss her book "Atlas of the Heart." And I want to live in reality.

Fantasy living, albeit a fun distraction for a time, can quickly feel empty and vapid. And when I'm desperately clinging to something that isn't real, I quickly understand that I'm compounding the struggle when I don't accept it. I am also unable to experience the contentment that comes with moving a little farther along the path of self-understanding.

I have come to understand that although I will always be in process, there are beautiful places to rest along the way, turnouts on a winding mountain road where I can pause and take in the breathtaking vistas. I recently rested at such a precipice to appreciate the growth I have experienced in my life.

I am looking out over the view of my life so far and see a more complete, centered self in the middle of my being, a self that has been forming over decades, and I like what I see. This is growth.

So, I am ready to declare from the rooftops: Fine! Life's a Journey!

I will take every opportunity to enjoy the view when I can. And when I am distracted by achy feet, tired of walking, I will find comfort in knowing I'm not alone.

Fling

(First published in Remington Review, Summer 2022)

"Let's go to this little place not far from here. I'll drive us," Danny says as we pay the bill after our meal. I'm enjoying the lingering Greek spices and the last tang from expertly paired wine as we deliberate about our next move.

My husband and I exchange looks. He is working in the morning and spontaneity is tricky when he has to be up before the crack of dawn to get to the fire station. His call.

"We're in!" he says with unexpected enthusiasm so we climb into our friend's car and drive to a hole-in-the-wall bar tucked in the corner of a strip mall a few miles away. I'm glad we're staying out, eager to sluff off the remaining heaviness from the funeral I watched via live stream earlier in the day. I'm happy to stay with our friends and keep the other challenges of the week at bay for a little longer.

"FLING. Open from 6 am to 2 am" the sign reads.

"Would love to see the 6 AM crowd," Carrie, Danny's

wife, says as we follow them to the door. I wonder what happens in the four hours of gap time when this place isn't open.

Once inside we walk back in time into a dimly lit room, walls covered in burgundy velvet brocade wallpaper on which are hung faded oil paintings of scantily clad women. Intricately patterned red carpeting completes the décor. Only the flat-screen TVs tucked in the corners over the bar suggest any modern upgrades.

We step into a space readymade for forgetting or escaping and settle into a half-booth with an unobstructed view of the band setting up on a stage ringed with a counter and Naugahyde barstools. Like a sushi bar, but in place of a chef there is a singer.

"Ragdoll" reads the banner to the left of the bassist's head, a gray-haired man warming up for the first set.

The lead singer, a woman draped in a long flowing caftan with dark gray curly hair crowned by a small tiara, begins to welcome the room.

"Any Fling virgins here tonight?" she yells out and our table erupts as two of us raise our hands. We are not alone but there aren't many others, only a few other virgins scattered around the bar and we cheer for them too.

Most of the patrons have settled into what looks like familiar seats, greeting one another at neighboring tables. I wonder if they're locals in this watering hole, ready for an easy evening, ready to leave their troubles at the door.

As the band continues warming up for the opening song, we sip our first round of drinks and enjoy the people watching, me leaning back into the booth feeling the vodka loosen the weight of the past week. The funeral was a poignant mark on a week laden with reminders of the mental health crises many of my students are navigating as they re-enter the world of being in person with actual people.

They come into the classroom with stories of depression and social anxiety and family loss, which adds a necessary layer to my teaching. An added dimension that requires great care as I attempt to impart knowledge while also holding the experiences they bring with them into our space. I have walked students to the counseling center, started class with breathing exercises, and encouraged them to share a little with one another about how they are doing. But at the end of the days, when I am driving home, I am weary, saddened by the burdens they are carrying. Burdens like the ones carried by the 21-year old man whose funeral I watched earlier in the day.

I imagine seeing my students' faces coming around the corner by the juke-box at Fling's entry, escaping into the warmth of this place.

Across the room, a couple with arms draped over one another have begun to sway back and forth before the music even begins, already struggling to keep one another upright. I watch those two as a warning reminder to pay attention to the siren call of the cocktails that promise to dull the feelings. I don't want to suffer tomorrow and I sip my drink slowly. But the tingling in my body is already loosening my shoulders and widening my smile as the music starts to play, songs from the 70s, from our childhoods. With the first notes, we are dancing in our seats, singing along at the top of our lungs.

At "Brown Eyed Girl" Carrie gets up to dance in front of our table, grooving from side to side, arms stretched out above her, snapping along. She too is ready for a distraction after moving her father, now a widower with Parkinson's, into her home. She has become a reluctant participant in the crash course of the sandwich generation, learning to juggle both the care of her teenagers with the needs of her father. Sipping gin and dancing to Ragdoll seems to be helping a little.

More people trickle in, dodging the dancers, to hug a man with a long blonde ponytail, at the helm of a small soundboard in front of us. One of the newcomers smiles at the octogenarian in an all-leather ensemble, jacket, and pants with a spaghetti-strapped camisole. I watch a man in a red tank top head-bang like he is hearing death metal and not the likes of Fleetwood Mac coming from the bandstand. A short woman with a salt-and-pepper mullet sporting a Ragdoll t-shirt makes passing hellos as she moves to take a seat near the band and casually straddles a stool, surveying the room like she is the mayor of the place.

"Oh!" Carrie exclaims. "This was my dad's favorite song when I was growing up! He used to sing this to us around the house," she says as Ragdoll plays the first notes of Beast of Burden. She mouths the words, lost in memories very different from the new chapter that has started this week in her house. Could we go get him? I wonder.

I envision bringing him to Fling and a little magic happening that would strengthen his limbs such that he could ditch the walker and dance with his daughter, forgetting for just a little bit the loss of his wife, of his health, of his youth. Perhaps Carrie can play these old tunes for him later in the weekend.

When Carrie returns, we decide against another round of drinks. We settle in for one more song but our decision to extend the evening is now causing a little anxiety for my husband, the only one of us who has to work in the morning. It is difficult to extricate myself from this pause in the time-space continuum, but I slowly slide across the bench and walk to the exit. This visit to Fling did the trick, offering a little reprieve.

On the other side of the door is real life. Ragdoll plays us out.

To See What I Might Otherwise Miss

The sun hadn't appeared for weeks. My walk to the number 40 tram, the first leg of my three-part commute (tram, train, bus) to Klosterneuburg was chilling. In the eleven months of this routine, much of what I wanted to accomplish had been realized. I was uncomfortable, with a modicum of self-knowledge under my belt.

Then, it started to snow.

I had never seen a fully formed snowflake before. There was snow every winter of my childhood, but I had never actually seen a snowflake, like the cutouts made in kindergarten.

And there, in the middle of a cold, gray Austrian winter, resting on the sleeve of my green wool coat, were actual snowflakes. Resplendent in unique shapes. Each distinct from the others. Magnificent enough for me to stop and study them as they fell.

This was why I had come. To see what I might otherwise

miss.

It started as a dream, born out of anxiety around the question, "What are you going to do after you graduate?" At 21, I was finishing four years "nestled in the foothills of Montecito, California," words taken right from the school catalog. College was coming to its natural end.

As I moved through that final year, immersing myself in Rhetoric classes, enjoying frigid ocean swims, and sipping smoothies on a stone wall in front of The Biltmore Hotel, I often wondered, "What happens next?" Life had followed a logical course, with each step simply following the last one until that path culminated in college. And now college was ending. Next step unknown.

So, I began to dream. I crafted visions of what going abroad could look like, with options of working or serving somewhere, and I formulated a plan. My dad, himself a world traveler with connections through his counseling in different countries, helped me put out the word that I was a soon-to-be college graduate eager to work in another country.

Bright-eyed and optimistic, I was dreaming unburdened. Vision and possibility fueled this lofty plan to intentionally disrupt my comfort zone and expand my borders.

There was also a great desire to test all I had learned academically, spiritually, and personally. If the first 21 years of my life had been planned and generally straightforward, I was ready to create a new road, one with curves and turns. And if advice from elders was worth heeding, my 20s were the time to do it, before life's responsibilities tethered me in place.

I sent my letters of inquiry. I put out feelers through various organizations. I graduated and prepared for my cross-country trek home to Virginia.

I received no word from abroad.

With a diploma in hand and all my college belongings crammed into a powder blue '82 Honda Accord, a friend and I traveled the 10 Eastbound through the South. Two weeks of freedom, without rules or phones (1994) or any idea of the future beyond the job I had waiting for me at my dad's office.

We played cassette tapes (my collection including an album by the 10,000 Maniacs, which was mistaken for heavy metal in Texarkana by a nice guy our age who noticed the name while assisting us at the gas station) and took in the wide-open spaces.

Disoriented and continuing to grapple with "now what," I fell in with a group of people all trying to find our footing as we acclimated to post-college life in our 20s.

A few months after graduation, during one long afternoon, wading through filing, I picked up a call for my dad from his friend in Vienna, Austria. The man was responding to one of my inquiries and wondered if I was available to work for him.

In Austria. For a year. Dream realized. Fall, 1994.

By mid-January, most of the details arranged, housing secured, I was ready to board a plane. My vision for the year included not only expanding my horizons but also creating enough friction in my inner world to disrupt complacency, remove blind spots, test my worldview.

Ah, the grandiose dreamer.

I can still see my 22-year-old self in vivid color. Brown curly hair just above my shoulders. Peach wool sweater over tan pants. Tear-stained face as I hug my parents in Dulles airport, ready to embark on a 12-month adventure; a year that will include me gazing in awe one cold morning at individual snowflakes falling on my coat.

Twenty-six years have passed.

Now 48, with a husband, two kids and a mortgage, boarding planes for a year is not on my calendar. But there are whispers in the back of my mind that remind me of those days so many years ago, when it seems like one chapter is ending and a new one beginning. When the question, "What next?" visits me from time to time.

The beginning and ending are more nebulous now. Not as concrete. But I find myself wondering, was that the only time to dream big? Is it too late now, with middle-age a concrete reality? Can I dream unfettered like this again?

Perhaps it's time to make a few inquiries; open myself to new dreams.

And in dreaming, I again hope to see what I might otherwise miss.

Quiet On My 50th Birthday

I am on the couch under a ridiculously soft blanket. The dog is curled next to me quietly snoring as "Chill Holiday" music plays. The fire is crackling, it is cold for Southern California. And I am basking in so much good.

For, you see, today is my 50th birthday. And I have been celebrating and marking this occasion since November 1, starting with a 50-day writing marathon to write 50 essays up to my 50th birthday.

December is generally a wild mix of end-of-semester tasks, birthdays and holidays. There is very little time to pause, sit quietly, and reflect. However, with this milestone birthday now upon me, it seemed extra important to carve out time for just that, pause, sit quietly, and reflect.

And I'm finding it is quite magical.

It is also discombobulating, uncomfortable, anxiety-producing, and befuddling. There is a reason I haven't chosen to sit quietly in a while because I know that under the surface is bubbling a lot of emotions I'm not always comfortable feeling.

Lately, in the midst of all the celebrating and joy, I have been extra-agitated, short with my children, and a little prone to, ahem, road rage. These are not things I want to feel during the holidays. Certainly not on this big birthday. I have come to know that these are symptoms of other things stirring in my soul.

So, today, on my birthday, I have chosen to sit and see what emerges from within, no matter what it is.

And there are tears. (Nothing violent or distressing. I have mastered containing feelings of sadness and grief, feeling much more comfortable in anger.) Today, however, I am trying to let the tears emerge and they are pointing to a whole host of things.

First, is the overwhelmed awareness that I am loved. Deeply. I am not entirely sure why this takes so long to sink in. Perhaps because powerful love can be staggering, disorienting, suspicious. I wonder why there is so much love coming at me.

If people only knew...

But what I'm learning is that my people do know...and they love me in all of it, the shit I carry deep inside myself.

This is enough to flatten a person. It is enough to bring tears, especially on one's 50th birthday.

The tears are also telling me that it is okay to feel uncertain about aging, that getting older is about holding mystery. It's precarious. And this can be scary. I also know that whatever denial I held in my 30s and 40s about being a full-blown adult is now completely exposed. There is no question that I am not only an adult but entering the older side of adulthood. It is a humbling awareness. It is a humbling journey.

This leads to tears of gratitude. I am so profoundly grateful that I'm on the journey at all. I have said goodbye to friends way too early in their lives. And this grief breeds humbling awareness that I have the privilege to keep going.

This has all been stirring in my spirit for the last few months and I knew there would be a time when it was important, maybe even imperative, to settle myself in. And sit. Quietly. And feel it all.

What I didn't expect was the magic in it, the transformative experience of honoring one's self and feelings. I didn't expect to feel cleansed and healed and whole in this moment.

I am also one who is often tempted to make this a conclusion. For example, I am finally cleansed and healed and whole, full stop. No more growth needed. And this is also part of the magic, knowing this isn't the case. I have just turned off the road for a moment, at a vista point to look out over the view. At this moment I feel the cleansing and healing. And, when I'm ready, I will carry on with the journey.

In the next few days, the journey will include wrapping and baking and organizing as I ready our house for Christmas day. These will be moments of magic for our family.

But today, right now, the magic is for me alone in this quiet moment, by the fire, with the dog, and my tears.

The Wood Song

Having just turned 50, I find myself in a period of deep reflection, looking back over the journey that has gotten me to this point. I have lost some things and gained some things. I have collected things and archived others.

I'm evaluating valuable messages and considering the truths that will carry me through this milestone birthday and into the decade that follows. I have been thinking about songs and shows and books and podcasts that have been the most influential in the last 49 years, and one song consistently tops these lists.

It's a song that when it comes on my streaming playlists there is no choice but to turn the volume up and sing at the top of my lungs. Tears inevitably accompany the music. I have this experience with many of the Indigo Girls' songs, who transcend time with their wisdom and lyricism.

But one of their songs makes me pause, contemplate, and examine life in a deeply profound way, *The Wood Song*.

When *The Wood Song* was released in 1994, I was preparing to graduate college, wondering what the next chapter held. The only certainty was packing up my '82 blue Honda hatchback and driving across the country back to Virginia from California where I spent four years matriculating at a small college in the hills of Santa Barbara.

I was ready to leave the Ivory Tower, ready to say goodbye to California forever. I certainly didn't know that in just five years, after some time working as a receptionist for my dad, 18 months living in Austria, and two years working on Capitol Hill, I would return to California to marry my fiancé and settle in for the rest of my adult life on the West Coast.

In 1994 I was asking the familiar question of the newly graduated, "What now?" and listening to these lyrics play on my cassette tape *Swamp Ophelia*.

The thin horizon of a plan is almost clear
My friends and I have had a tough time
Bruising our brains hard up against change
All the old dogs and the magician
Now I see we're in the boat in two by twos
Only the heart that we have for a tool we could use
And the very close quarters are hard to get used to
Love weighs the hull down with its weight
But the wood is tired and the wood is old
And we'll make it fine if the weather holds
But if the weather holds we'll have missed the point
That's where I need to go.

I remember singing the words, "We'll make it fine if the weather holds. But if the weather holds, we'll have missed the point," and thinking whatever is in front of me, I want the certainty of calm seas and good weather.

I didn't like the idea that good weather meant I would have missed the point, which I interpreted as meaning it is only with rough seas, high winds, and storms that one is honed and strengthened into becoming who I thought I wanted to be, a strong, resilient, and successful woman.

At the time I was also more tied to the belief in a higher power rooted in a faith I had cultivated and grown for much of my life. I was comforted by the words that said I was watched over. Regardless of what life held, I rested in believing someone, a "greater hand," was watching closely over my journey.

No way construction of this tricky plan
Was built by other than a greater hand
With a love that passes all our understanding
Watching closely over the journey

In my twenties, I returned from overseas, met the man I was to marry, uprooted myself once again, and settled into a new life in a dorm overseeing college students. I began to realize that the journey, with all its unpredictable twists and turns, required a certain fortitude I *said* I wanted in theory, but in practice realized I wanted a much easier road.

When the song played again, now on a CD copy of *Swamp Ophelia* from my husband's collection, I began wondering if the Indigo Girls were right. Is the prize always worth the rocky ride? And what is the prize, exactly? And do I have the courage?

Yeah but what it takes to cross the great divide
Seems more than all the courage I can muster up inside
Although we get to have some answers when we reach the other side
The prize is always worth the rocky ride.

I considered the courage required to cross the great divide, which I had come to interpret as life, when my husband and I realized having biological children would require more than intercourse. Based on my years-long struggle with endometriosis, we would need medical intervention if I wanted to get pregnant.

The years of infertility and in vitro fertilization required a courage I didn't know I had until I was already on the road. That is one thing about courage. Sometimes we don't know how much of it we possess until we are suddenly in the middle of life's circumstances.

I would further reflect on how much courage I could muster when our second round of implanting embryos resulted in the birth of a beautiful, healthy baby boy with Down Syndrome.

We knew this diagnosis before he was born and the news once again called me to tap into my courage reserves. I was thankful to find there was some available. That's another thing about courage. Sometimes it sits in great quantities, like a water supply at the bottom of a well. Other times it is available in small drips like an IV of carefully measured fluids.

Now, squarely in middle age, I find myself returning to this song and chuckling at the truth of the next lyric. I marvel at the folly of thinking this would even be possible because I know life doesn't work this way.

But still, I hope that perhaps I might get some hints of what the road ahead holds for me ,and maybe I can "steer clear" of some of the bumps and potholes. It helps me to know that two older, wiser women have already acknowledged this understandable human desire and "its futility."

Sometimes I ask to sneak a closer look
Skip to the final chapter of the book
And then maybe steer us clear from some of the pain it took
To get us where we are this far yeah
But the question drowns in its futility
And even I have got to laugh at me
No one gets to miss the storm of what will be
Just holding on for the ride.

So, I settle in. On the harder days, I play the song again, now from my Pandora streaming service through a Bluetooth speaker. And I try to hold on for the ride.

The wood is tired and the wood is old
We'll make it fine if the weather holds
But if the weather holds we'll have missed the point
That's where I need to go.

Rejection is Real

I used to think people were kidding, specifically people like writers and coaches and editors, who were continually reminding us new, wide-eyed novice writers that rejection is real. I didn't realize just how much I doubted these wise voices. I mean, in theory, I accepted their words as important guidelines to remember as I embarked on the journey of publishing essays. If I were in face-to face conversations with them, I would have nodded, with serious and humble acknowledgement that what they were sharing was very important.

But underneath this surface-level agreement I nurtured optimism that either I wouldn't experience the same level of rejection or that I *would* experience a lot of rejection but I wouldn't let it get to me. I would keep marching toward my publishing goals.

It's getting to me.

After receiving my thirtieth hard pass since my first dip into publishing, I am trying to cling to any sign of hope I can. But I now realize rejection is real. Very real. And it doesn't feel great. But I'm not flattened. I'm still marching. Looking for alternative options.

Perhaps that is the most important element in all of the sage advice I have sought out and read on my writing journey: keep marching towards the goal. And for me, marching means writing.

I am motivated to do this for several reasons. First, although I have been writing for a decade, my fear of rejection has kept me from even stepping into the publishing arena, a place I would like to be.

As Brene Brown quotes, and quotes often, an excerpt from Teddy Roosevelt's speech "Citizenship in the Republic" from which she named her book "Daring Greatly," we can't expect any success if we don't jump into the arena in the first place.

"It is not the critic who counts; not the man who points out how the strong [person] stumbles, or where the doer of deeds could have done them better. The credit belongs to the [person] who is actually in the arena, whose face is marred by dust and sweat and blood; who strives valiantly; who errs; who comes short again and again, [Read: Rejection] because there is no effort without error and shortcoming; but who does actually strive to do the deeds; who knows great enthusiasms, the great devotions; who spends [her]self in a worthy cause; who at the best knows in the end the triumph of high achievement, and who at the worst, if [she] fails, at least fails while daring greatly. . ."

For many years I didn't even park in the parking lot of the arena. I drove to a nearby hillside and looked at the arena from a distance, through binoculars. Then, a few years ago I drove closer to the arena and camped out in a little coffee shop called "WordPress" and with the help of my sister-in-law, started a blog.

Still not *in* the arena.

Baby steps.

Then, I drove to the arena. But I took some friends with me. They walked with me to the large doors that led onto the field, cheering and clapping as I took my steps into the center of it, ready to more formally release my words out into the ether.

At this point it is imperative to pause and note the power of community when we head to the arena. I have many significant voices in my life, cheerleaders, who say "You've got this!" "Keep going!" "We'll bring wine when you get rejected!"

These people are important.

Although the actual daring greatly must be done from one's own agency, it doesn't mean we can't bring people with us. My parents, my friends, mastermind group, and coach didn't carry me in. They didn't write the words for me. They didn't berate me for how slowly I was moving towards my publishing goals. They were there for my first steps, and keep cheering as I continue to stay in the arena.

But, even when I can see my supporters over there in the entryway, it can be lonely in the arena, writing, submitting, and reading rejection emails. We writers know this intimately. I imagine a stand-up comic in front of a skeptical audience or a gladiator waiting for lions to be released or a rookie pitcher coming to the mound for the first time and as each of these figures turns to the crowd there might be flowers or tomatoes thrown at their feet.

There might be loud boos or simply apathy. But they stay in the space.

It is interesting that even if flowers are thrown or encouragement shouted, it is usually the tomatoes that are remembered. I have received two "yes's" from literary magazines, for which I jumped up and down and called all my cheerleaders. But it is difficult to remember those yes's.

Perhaps I should bring wins with me into the arena, stake them in the ground on signposts as reminders of what I hope to accomplish and why I am still standing here. Or, after short breaks, why I keep returning.

I applaud we who continue to come back again and again, entering the arena regardless of the rejections. I applaud we who stay to throw our words into the ether.

I applaud we who are in the arena.

To Dear Friends

A friend of mine recently remarked, or rather I should say, a DEAR friend of mine recently remarked that I often describe my friends as dear. Apparently I do this a lot. This friend's observation prompted me to think more about what this word "dear" means and what are the qualities embodied in those dear friends I'm so fond of mentioning.

A dear friend is thoughtful, kind, and magnanimous. She is wise and curious. He is ready with questions about the journey of life and open to sharing personal stories. Dear friends are mentors, teachers, creators, and guides. They inspire me to listen, learn, share, laugh, give, and receive.

Dear friends come to readings even if they don't know what a reading is. They support my marriage and hold space for my boys. They hold special space for my special boy.

They show me how to laugh at things that don't need to

be taken so seriously. And they listen seriously when I can't laugh. They talk about podcasts and then they make talking about podcasts a drinking game.

They share life and meals and walks and television shows and boats. They listen to incessant babbling about a cold plunge that is arriving shortly and then they test out that cold plunge even if their tits almost freeze off.

They come bundled up to sit in a backyard on a cold night to celebrate a milestone birthday.

And this is a great thing about aging, knowing what a gift it is to find one's life filled with such friends. Aging brings a deeper appreciation for the people with whom one has weathered the storms, shared the journey, sat in the ashes, and celebrated the triumphs. Getting older crystalizes the knowledge that these friends are treasures. They are precious. They are a gift and they are dear.

So, to my dear friends, thank you for all the things I listed above because, of course, I was talking about you. You teach me, shape me, love me as I am. You make me think and grow, flourish and thrive. It is a gift to do life with you. I am honored and humbled to call each of you not just friend, but a DEAR friend.

Acknowledgements

I have read many acknowledgement pages and I am always amazed at the sheer volume of people it takes to make something like this happen. Now, that I'm crafting my own acknowledgements page, I am floored with gratitude for the people I get to do life with. I am so grateful for my community who cheers me on.

Writing this collection of essays began with my first blog and my sister-in-law, Jamie Osterhaus, who sat with me on the couch and patiently walked me through the details of setting it up, while repeating, "You can do this. You can do this. You can do this." Your enthusiasm has been a gift from the beginning. This book also begins with my brother, Ben, who has been my cheerleader and friend from day one and who's best feedback on my work usually starts with, "Dayum." It is a profound gift to have you both in my corner.

To my parents who have been celebrating my voice ever since I started putting it down on paper. Thank you for teaching me to examine the world around me with curiosity and empathy. I am deeply grateful for your love and support. Even at 50, I still bask in your pride and affirmation.

There have also been so many dear friends who have listened to me for years talk about publishing. Thank you to my mastermind group, Thrive, Cheryl Mathieu, Mary Van Geffen, Shelly Milsap, and Kimber Del Valle, for sitting with me and my tears, for reading my essays, and for encouraging me forward. And a special thank you to Kimber, who has been a writing mentor and partner for a very long time. Thank you for working with me on the practice and discipline of writing. I know being on the journey with you means I will continue to learn about the craziest things.

To Carrie and Danny Paschall, who have been fans from my first essay and hosted my first reading event, expanding my writing dreams by adding a microphone. Your friendship is energy, light, and a balm to my soul.

To Bronwen Newcott, a kindred spirit from the first moment she suggested we write together. Your creativity and gift for words inspire me in my own work and I'm thrilled to see where this writing adventure takes us.

To Korie Ebmeyer who contributed a significant piece of the publishing puzzle by asking one day a few years ago, "Have you heard of the website, Medium?"

To Cheryl Biber who has been a faithful reader of my work since I was writing for the PTA newsletter. I am so grateful for your support, your listening ear on our long dog walks, and for often being one of the first people to like an essay when I post it on social media. And to Jennifer Vickers and Darcy Grise, who listen to me wax on about my writing and always cheer for me to pursue my dream. Who knew when we all met as neighbors that we would one day become family?

Thank you to Chris Sowers who not only agreed to be my coach but has also been a dedicated voice in pushing me to meet my writing goals. Thank you so much for your work on this book, editing, formatting, and fielding all my questions about the minutiae. Working with you keeps me on track and encourages me to continue taking the next step. So grateful for you, coach.

To Andrea Bowers, a woman I am proud to call sister and friend, for her generous offer to do the cover. I was speechless then and I am speechless now at this gift or, dare I say, this radical generosity.

To my boys, it is a privilege to be your mom. I write about us so that I will not only be present in the moments of our life together but so that you will also see in these pages how much I love you. I am in awe of who you are and who you are becoming.

And to Jud, my life partner, thank you for honoring the place writing has in my life. Thank you for listening to many drafts of many essays. Thank you for helping orchestrate time and schedules so I can write. And thank you for reminding me of who I am when I forget. Ours is a partnership that continuously reminds me of the "power of two." We're gonna make it, I swear.

About the Cover Artist

Los Angeles-based artist Andrea Bowers (b. 1964, Ohio) has been recording and amplifying the work of activists present and past for more than two decades. Her multi-media practice includes drawing, video, sculpture, and installation work that foregrounds the experience of the people who dedicate their time and energy to the struggle for gender, racial, environmental, labor, and immigration justice and those who are directly affected by systemic inequality. Over time, her different bodies of work have become a document of the changing language, prerogatives, and dynamics of social justice movements. In 2021 a major mid—career survey of Bowers' work opened at the MCA Chicago and traveled to the Hammer Museum in Los Angeles in 2022.